AF600556

RESERVED BENEFICES

THE CATHOLIC UNIVERSITY OF AMERICA
CANON LAW STUDIES
NO. 161

RESERVED BENEFICES

BY THE
REV. JOHN J. HAYDT, A.B., J.C.L.
PRIEST OF THE ARCHDIOCESE OF PHILADELPHIA

A DISSERTATION

Submitted to the Faculty of Canon Law of the Catholic University of America in Partial Fulfillment of the Requirements for the Degree of

DOCTOR OF CANON LAW

WASHINGTON, D. C.
1942

Nihil Obstat:

Eduardus G. Roelker, S.T.D., J.C.D.,
Censor Deputatus

Washingtonii, D. C., die XX Maii 1942.

Imprimatur:

✠ D. Card. Dougherty,
Archiepiscopus Philadelphiensis

Philadelphiae, die XXI Maii 1942.

The Wickersham Printing Company
Lancaster, Pennsylvania

To My Mother

and to the

Memory of My Father

FOREWORD

The Church has always labored under the responsibility of appointing to benefices only such clerics who are capable of administering the power of orders and jurisdiction in accordance with the strict provisions of Canon Law. Ordinarily the duty of selecting proper candidates rests in the hands of the local ordinaries. Ultimately, however, this responsibility is part of the burden of the Roman Pontiff, who has been entrusted with the guidance of the entire Christian flock. In virtue of this supreme jurisdiction over the universal Church many of the Popes have taken some part in the conferring of benefices situated outside the diocese of Rome. Such participation is termed papal provisions. One of the forms of the papal provision is the reservation of a benefice. It is the purpose of this present work to offer a study of reserved benefices.

This study is divided into two sections, the one an historical synopsis and the other a canonical commentary. The former is primarily concerned with three distinct problems: first, the start of the system of reserved benefices; second, an attempt to evaluate the criticism often directed at this papal system; third, the sudden development and the slow decline of reserved benefices. To the reader it will probably seem that too much emphasis has been placed on the lay domination of churches and clergy during the ninth, tenth, and eleventh centuries. Such a detailed study is required, however, because only a most careful analysis of this situation discloses the answer to the important question, why did the Popes start reserving benefices.

The second section of this work consists principally of a commentary on canon 1435, which enumerates all the reservations in effect at the present time. For the fuller comprehension of the import of this canon it was found necessary to consider also the related questions of the right of the Pope to reserve benefices, of the legal nature of the reservation, of the conferring of reserved benefices, and of the reservations which obtain in the United States. This dissertation does not consider the effect of an act performed by one who holds a reserved benefice illegally. Such a consideration would be beyond the scope of this work. Merely the existence of reserved benefices and the effect of their reservation are considered here.

The author takes this occasion to express his sincere gratitude to His Eminence, Dennis Cardinal Dougherty, Archbishop of Philadelphia, for the opportunity of advanced study at the Catholic University of America, and his profound appreciation to all who in any way have assisted in the preparation of this work for their interest and kindness.

TABLE OF CONTENTS

CHAPTER X

CHAPTER XI

CHAPTER XII

CHAPTER XIII

PART I

HISTORICAL SYNOPSIS

CHAPTER I

Preliminary Discussion

ARTICLE 1. CONFERRING OF BENEFICES BY THE LOCAL ORDINARY

There is an *intentio in iure fundata* which favors the right of the local ordinary to confer all vacant benefices in his territory.[1] This *intentio in iure fundata* implies the same canonical effects as the presumption of law.[2] This provision of the Code is not new legislation. In fact, it represents one of the most ancient rules on the ecclesiastical benefice.[3] It is to be noted that the precise wording of this legal norm simply states the existence of a presumption of law favoring the local ordinary. It prescinds entirely from the question of the actual conferring of these benefices. Consequently to conclude that the ordinary of the place, in virtue of this ancient rule, has been conferring all the vacant benefices in his territory would be to misconstrue the force of the juridical presumption. Indeed the history of the Church reveals that it has been approximately fifteen centuries since such a practice prevailed.

During the life of the Church there have been two forces strong enough to overcome the force of this presumption of law—the papacy and the more powerful element of the laity. It must be admitted that at times the latter of these two factors acted with

[1] Canon 1432, § 1: "...Cardinalis in proprio titulo vel diaconia et Ordinarius loci in proprio territorio habent intentionem in iure fundatam."

[2] Coronata, *Institutiones iuris canonici*, vol. III (Taurini: Marietti, 1933), n. 1273.

[3] C. 6, X, *De exceptionibus*, II, 25: here Innocent III (1198-1216) upholds the claim of a bishop to the *intentio fundata* of conferring all vacant churches in his diocese. Long before the canonical benefices as such existed, the Church's system of relative ordinations implicitly favored the local bishops in the matter of conferring many ecclesiastical offices. For a consideration of this relative ordination, consult Joseph Weier, *Der Kanonische Weihetitel* (Würzburg: Richard Mayr, 1936).

perfect legality, exercising the power of the *ius patronatus*. More frequently, however, its action was illegal and was based, as the next chapter will show, either on greed for power or on the mistaken belief that a church was no different than any other building.

ARTICLE 2. CONFERRING OF BENEFICES BY THE POPES

The second factor which has restricted the right of the local ordinary in the conferring of vacant benefices has been the papacy. Whenever a Pope takes any active part whatever in the conferring of a benefice, e. g., by nominating a cleric for that office, that conferring is known as a papal provision.[4] Since papal provisions will be studied more thoroughly in another section of this dissertation, the treatment in this preliminary discussion will be limited to two points: first, the dispute about its origin and second, a brief summary of the various forms of papal provisions.

Concerning the question of papal provisions of ecclesiastical offices outside Rome there is one school which maintains that such conferrings appeared as early as the sixth and seventh centuries.[5] The other school of thought, however, insists that the Popes did not commence this practice of conferring benefices in the dioceses of other bishops until the year 1137.[6]

[4] For the extensive field of literature of this subject consult the bibliography in Barraclough, *Papal provisions* (Oxford: Basil Blackwell, 1935), pp. 179-187.

[5] Bouix, *Tractatus de principiis iuris canonici* (Parisiis, 1882), p. 182; Wernz-Vidal, *Ius canonicum* (7 toms. in 8 vols., Romae: Apud Aedes Universitatis Gregorianiae, 1923-1938), II, p. 247, n. 227; Thomassinus, *Vetus et nova Ecclesiae disciplina circa beneficia et beneficiarios* (3 vols., Lucae: L. Venturini, 1728), pars II, lib. I, c. 41, NN. 1-4.

[6] Hinschius, *System des katholischen Kirchenrechts* (4 vols., Berlin, 1869-1888), III, 114; Barraclough, *Papal provisions*, p. 4; Linden, *Der Tod des Benefiziaten in Rom* (Bonn: Ludwig Roehrscheid, 1938), p. 3. This work will be referred to hereafter simply as: Linden, *op. cit.* Mollat, *La collation des benefices ecclesiastiques sous les Papes d'Avignon* (Paris: Fontemoing & Cie., 1921), p. 42.

At times in the succeeding chapters of this work it may seem that the contention of this latter school is being upheld. Yet that is not the case. It is the intention of this writer to abstain from any preference for either of these opinions. The course adopted here is solely one of policy. This thesis will treat the vast system of reserved benefices, which in turn is but a part of the much more extensive system of papal provisions. Thus when it is stated in any of the succeeding chapters that the first papal provision appeared in 1137, the writer means that the practical start of the system of papal provisions occurred in this year. Interpreted in this light, this statement is acceptable to both schools, for the first school merely maintains that there were isolated examples of papal provisions in the earlier centuries.[7]

Once this practical system of papal provisions was under way, the actions of the Popes assumed one of four forms. As the next chapter will show in detail, the Popes at first merely advised and *counseled* the local ordinaries to confer a given benefice on a particular cleric. In the second stage, which appeared almost simultaneously with the first,[8] a command was issued in this regard. The next step found the Popes themselves conferring the benefices. Under the first and simplest form of this third type of papal provisions the Popes conferred vacant benefices before the local bishops conferred them. The second form of this direct conferring, the form which provides the topic of this dissertation, was the reservation of the benefice. Here the Popes withdrew the power over the benefice from all inferior collators and reserved the right of conferring it to themselves.[9] The reservation is commonly defined as the act whereby the Pope withdraws to

[7] Wernz-Vidal, *Ius canonicum*, II, 247: "...Romani Pontifices...officiorum ecclesiasticorum quandoque suam interposuerunt auctoritatem..."

[8] Wernz-Vidal, *Ius canonicum*, II, 248.

[9] For a more detailed study of these four types of papal provisions consult Barraclough, *Papal provisions*, pp. 8, ff. and Ioannes de Selua, *Tractatus de beneficio* (no place, 1513), pars II, q. I, n. 8.

himself the power to confer a benefice which is about to become vacant.[10]

ARTICLE 3. APPROACH TO THE HISTORICAL BACKGROUND OF RESERVED BENEFICES

It is from the more general aspect of papal provisions that the view will be sketched of the historical background which nurtured the birth and growth of reserved benefices. Great stress will be laid on this background, so great indeed that some explanation is in order for this departure from the usual canonical treatment.

The traditional non-Catholic presentation of papal provisions has judged this system as completely corrupt. This view conceives the system of papal provisions as the most flagrant example of papal greed. With the turn of the century, however, there has been an appreciable tendency to depart from such a view.[11] This tendency is the direct result of considering the thirteenth, fourteenth and fifteenth centuries in a direct line from the tenth, eleventh, and the twelfth centuries.[12] With this in mind much of the attention of this work shall be focused on these earlier centuries. Not only will the base accusations concerning the start of papal provisions be investigated and refuted, but it will also be shown that many of the later accusations against this system should be seriously questioned.

[10] Riganti, *Commentaria in regulas, constitutiones, et ordinationes cancellariae apostolicae* (opus posthumum, 4 vols. in 2, Coloniae Allobrogum, 1751), ad regul. I, pars I, n. 31. In the future this work will be referred to simply as Riganti; Linden, *op. cit.*, p. 14; Lux, *Collectio Constitutionum apostolicarum de generali beneficiorum reservatione ab anno 1265 usque ad annum 1378* (Wratislaviae: Müller & Scheiffert, 1904), p. 4. In the future this work will be referred to simply as Lux.

[11] Barraclough, *Papal provisions*, p. 57: "Such a judgment as this cuts right across the old fashioned estimate of provisions as an instrument of papal greed and unscrupulous materialism . . ."

[12] Barraclough, *op. cit.*, p. 59.

CHAPTER II

Historical Background

Article 1. The Proprietary Church

At the end of the Roman Epoch the canon law of the Church had deposited with the local bishops the power of conferring all churches within their territories. With the Christianization of the Germanic peoples, however, and the ensuing infiltration of their influence over the European Continent a new order gradually evolved. This despite the fact that the ecclesiastical legislation on this point remained unaltered.

This policy of extreme transition in the administration of ecclesiastical appointments had its root in the early Germanic concept of property as applied to a church, the *Eigenkirchenwesen.* Literally this would be translated as the system of owned churches. The more acceptable English equivalent is the system of *proprietary churches.*

According to this early Germanic concept a church was devoid of all juristic personality. It was a thing, an object.[1] Whoever owned the land, owned the church as well.[2] He could sell it in whole or in part, exchange it or give it away.[3] Any profit which

[1] U. Stutz, "The proprietary church as an element of medieval Germanic ecclesiastical law"—Vol. II of *Medieval German essays,* translated by G. Barraclough, pp. 35-70 (Oxford: Basil Blackwell, 1938), p. 41.

[2] Capitulary of Lothaire I in the year 824, c. 2—"Si quis homo liber per consensum episcopi sui ecclesiam in sua construxerit proprietate ..." —*MGH, Leges,* I (ed. by Pertz, Leipzig, reprinted in 1925), 236. Hincmar of Rheims (d. 882), *Litterae canonicae*: "... ecclesias in proprietatibus hominum ..."—Migne, *Patrologiae cursus completus,* series Latina, (221 vols., Parisiis, 1844-1864), CXXVI, 274. Hereafter cited *MPL.*

[3] Agobard, Bishop of Lyons (d. 840), *Liber de dispensatione ecclesiasticarum rerum* (828): "Nunc non solum possessiones ecclesiae sed etiam ipsae ecclesiae cum possessionibus vendantur."—*MPL,* CIV, 238. Capi-

accrued to the church was his.[4] It is generally contended that the church owners *de facto* hired and dismissed their clerics as they pleased.[5] The truth of this statement is rather clearly reflected in the numerous prohibitions against this evil.[6]

This new order made its appearance in the Church as early as the sixth century. Thus the III Council of Braga (572) in Spain mentions the construction of churches for profit.[7] In the middle of the next century a vehement denunciation against the usurpations of the lay magnates was registered by the bishops at the Synod of Chalon-sur-Sâone (650).[8] This young movement gained surprising momentum and by the middle of the eighth century, " the victory of the proprietary church regime within the Frankish reign was decisive and this victory assured its entry into the legal system of the Western Church." [9]

The precise percentage of the churches affected by this system naturally remains unknown. Certainly it was the majority of the churches. Imbart de la Tour in his reliable work on the

tulary of Charlemagne in the year 794, c. 54: " De ecclesiis quae ab ingenuis hominibus construuntur, liceat eas tradere vel vendere ... "—*MGH, Leges*, I, 75.

[4] Stutz, " The proprietary church "—*Medieval German essays*, p. 42.

[5] Wernz-Vidal, *Ius canonicum*, II, 292; Fischer, *The medieval empire* (2 vols., London, 1898), II, 67; Coronata, *Institutiones iuris canonici*, II, n. 1,000.

[6] E. g., c. 29, Council of Mainz (813)—*MGH, Legum Sectio III, Concilia*, tom. II, pars I, p. 265; Capitulary decree of the year 819, n. 8, *MGH, Legum, Sectio II, Capitularia Regum Francorum*, tom. I, p. 277.

[7] C. 6: " Placuit ut si quis basilicam non pro devotione fidei sed pro quaestu cupiditatis aedificat, ut quidquid ibidem de oblatione populi ibidem colligitur, medium cum clericis dividat ... "—Mansi, IX, 840.

[8] C. 14: " ... quod oratoria per villas potentum iam longo constructa tempore ac facultates ibidem collatas, ipsi quorum villae sunt, episcopis contradicant et iam ipsos clericos, qui ad ipsa oratoria deserviunt, ab archidiacono coerceri permittant."—*MGH, Legum Sectio III, Concilia*, tom. I, *Concilia Aevi Merovingici* (ed. by F. Maasen, Hannoveriae, 1893).

[9] Stutz, " The proprietary church "—*Medieval German essays*, p. 42.

Eigenkirche estimates that almost all the churches were proprietary.[10]

The attitude adopted by the clergy towards this change in the administration of the churches was none too aggressive. For one thing, as the preceding footnote illustrates, many of the bishops themselves owned churches. Nevertheless there were sporadic outbursts of bitter opposition.[11] Furthermore these same expressions of hostility to the lay domination of ecclesiastical offices appeared with sufficient frequency to show that the approval of the Church was not forthcoming.

It would not prove difficult to imagine the havoc and disaster wrought by this system on the Church. To the average landowner, the church was little more than a financial investment (usually classified as one of the best investments of the Middle Ages). His primary interest was profit. The essential requirement he demanded of his hired cleric was a sharp business acumen, especially the ability to collect the tithes and miscellaneous fees. He was not concerned with the spirituality or the learning of his cleric. He tended to encourage the disobedience of the latter towards his bishop. The simony which resulted from this evil must have been most common.[12] In all, it was a sad scene with reference to the conferring of the churches.

What about the influence of this *Eigenkirchenwesen* on the bishoprics? Stutz is essentially correct when he concludes that

[10] *De ecclesiis rusticanis aetate carolingica* (Burdegalae, 1890), p. 137: "...ecclesiae fere omnes, decimo saeculo, dominum proprium senioremve sive episcopum sive laicum, habuerunt, quae venduntur, donantur, pignorantur, quin etiam inter multos cohaeredes dividi solent."

[11] Cc. 3, 4 of the German Council of 742—*MGH, Legum Sectio III, Concilia*, tom. II, pars I (ed. by A. Werminghoff, Berlin, 1904), p. 3; Bishop Agobard of Lyons, *loc. cit.*; canon 9 of the Council of Valence in the year 855—*Mansi*, XV, 8.

[12] C. 5, Council of Arles (813): "...ut laici omnino a presbyteris non audeant exigere propter commendationem ecclesiae; quia plerumque propter cupiditatem a laicis..."—*MGH, Legum Sectio III, Concilia*, tom. II, pars I, p. 25. Canon 15 of the Council of Tours (813) describes the practice of priests buying churches as "vitium late diffusum."—*MGH, ibid.*, p. 288.

the possibility of reducing the bishoprics to the position of real private (proprietary) churches could be realized only in unusually favorable circumstances.[13] There was a good reason for this barrier. From early times the kings had bestowed on the bishops numerous favors and privileges regarding secular affairs. Gradually the position of the bishop became an important one in the civil government. Naturally the kings expected something in return. In this case the exaction was the control of the episcopal election.

Parsons notes the appearance of this interference as early as the sixth century.[14] By the eighth century this imperial interference had developed into an institution.[15] In summarizing the episcopal elections of the eleventh century J. Bury presents the conservative appraisal: "In all these lands (Germany, France, and England) the decisive voice, indeed the real appointment itself, lay with the kings; the part played by others was small and varying."[16]

For our purpose that practically completes the treatment of the lay domination of ecclesiastical offices and benefices from the sixth to the eleventh centuries. During the last part of this period the laity was unquestionably the predominant factor in the conferring of churches. It was to this laity that most of the evils of the clergy could be traced. One last point that may here be added is the lay investiture. The investiture itself was an imitation of the ceremony by which a secular fief was conferred on an individual. It was any external manifestation, e. g., the handing of a ring to the recipient, to show that the lay owner was conferring on the cleric of his choice some office to which was at-

[13] "The proprietary church," pp. 62, 63.

[14] *Canonical elections,* Catholic University of America Canon Law Studies, n. 118 (Washington, D. C.: Catholic University Press, 1940), p. 41.

[15] Imbart de la Tour, *Les elections episcopales dans l'Eglise de la France du IXe au XIIe siecle* (Paris, 1890), p. 106.

[16] *Cambridge medieval history* planned by J. Bury and edited by Gwatkin and Whitney (8 vols., New York: Macmillan, 1911-1936), V, 6.

tached an ecclesiastical benefice. It is important to point out that this investiture was used not only for conferring bishoprics, but also for conferring minor benefices.

ARTICLE 2. THE CAROLINGIAN AND GREGORIAN REFORMS

In this section the reader will find a concise study of the inefficacy of the Carolingian Reform and of the relative success of the lay investiture struggle. In this manner the reforms attempted by the kings and by the Popes will be studied. The other reform movements, e. g., of Agobardus and of the Pseudo-Isidore Collections are only of minor import.

Several emperors of the Carolingian dynasty were zealous in the cause of reform. They were deeply concerned with the prevalent abuses of the clergy. In an effort to eradicate these abuses, they established schools, favored the celibacy of the clergy, and revised their legal systems so that the clergy should once more be subject to their bishops.

At the end of the Carolingian Reform, however, the condition of the clergy was just as poor as it had been. As several historians have remarked, that is the only result which could be logically expected of this movement. The Carolingians, as the largest proprietors of the owned churches, were vitally concerned in the maintenance of this system.[17] Consequently not one of their efforts was directed at the root of all the trouble.

With the failure of the highest lay authority to effect a reform of the clergy all hope was placed in the papacy. In the eleventh century the papacy placed the first acts of the Gregorian Reform, called after its most ardent exponent, Gregory VII (1073-1085).[18] Though the more general details of this Reform are sufficiently well known, it will prove helpful to recall the two following principles: first, the distinction between the investiture struggle

[17] Stutz, "The proprietary church," p. 47; Fischer, *The medieval empire,* II, 255.

[18] For a critical bibliography consult Thomas Oestrich, "The Hildebrandine Reform and its latest historian"—*Catholic Historical Review,* XII (1931-1932), 256-261.

and the Gregorian Reform, and secondly, the change in the papal policy after the death of Gregory.

The lay investiture struggle was distinct from the Gregorian Reform being but a part of the latter. This can be illustrated by an example. If a crowd of men are defacing a building by smearing paint on the walls, it will be one thing to chase the men away and another thing to restore the building to its former beauty. The lay investiture contest aimed merely at the removal of the lay interference in the conferring of benefices.

A sharp contrast existed between Gregory's plan of reform and the plan adopted by his successors. Gregory was bitterly opposed to all lay domination, whether over the bishoprics or over the lowly country church. This was the general tone of his famous condemnation of the lay investiture of bishops and lesser dignities by any superior, duke, marquis, count, or any temporal ruler.[19] This spirit was even more evident in other synods held under Gregory's auspices.[20] After Gregory's death, however, a spirit of compromise was at once noticeable. The lay investiture struggle was concerned only with the bishoprics. For the other churches a new policy was adopted. The attack now changed into the slow and gradual transformation of the *Eigenkirchenwesen* into the *ius patronatus*.[21] Even in this restricted contest against the lay investiture of bishoprics the new policy admitted a compromise, for the first great victory at the Concordat of Worms in 1122 [22] was essentially a compromise.

Yet the Concordat of Worms must be recognized as a victory for the Church. Even more important it signified that the Church was wresting from the laity the power over the benefices.

[19] Lenten Synod of 1075—*MGH, Scriptores, Hugh of Flavigny* (ed. by Pertz, Leipzig, 1848), VIII, 412.

[20] C. 1, Council of Poitiers (1078)—Mansi, XX, 498; c. 2, Roman Synod (1078)—Mansi, XX, 509; c. 2, Roman Synod (1080)—Mansi, XX, 532.

[21] Wernz-Vidal, *Ius canonicum*, II, 293, 294.

[22] *MGH, Legum Sectio*, IV, *Constitutiones et acta publica Regum*, I (edited by L. Weiland, 1892), 159-161.

But what was to be done with this power which was being reclaimed by the Church? In the answer to that question lies the necessity of papal provisions.

ARTICLE 3. THE NECESSITY OF PAPAL PROVISIONS

With the Church making appreciable strides in its restriction of lay domination, one may well question whether any progress was being made in the reform of the clergy. The analytic consideration of this question will be confined to the situation in Germany, which was typical of the conditions in the other countries. With the Concordat of Worms some advance had been made against the lay domination of bishops. Furthermore there is reason to believe that inroads were also being made on the *Eigenkirchenwesen.* But this power, which had been snatched from the laity, was being transferred for the greater part to the German clergy, especially to the hierarchy. Now that same hierarchy was the product of several centuries of lay domination. Their appointments had usually been political and often simoniacal.[23]

The Pontiffs of the Gregorian Reform placed little trust in them. Gregory himself commented on the episcopacy of his day: "When I review in my mind the regions of the West, whether north or south, I find scarce any bishops who lived or were ordained according to the law and who govern Christian people in the love of Christ and not for worldly ambition." [24] Even more revealing was the action of the German hierarchy after the Treaty of Sutri in the year 1111.[25] On February 12 of that year Paschal II (1099-1118) and Henry V (1106-1125) reached an agreement on the investiture problem which was quite favorable

[23] Albers, *Enchiridion historiae ecclesiasticae universae* (3rd ed., 3 vols., Neomagi, 1910), II, 47.

[24] *MGH, Epistolae,* tom. II, Fasciculus I, *Registrum Gregorii VII* (edited by E. Caspar, Berlin, 1920), 199. English translation from Agnes Cavanagh, *Pope Gregory and the theocratic state* (Washington, D. C.: Catholic University of America, 1934), p. 61.

[25] *MGH, Leges,* II, pp. 66-69.

to the Church. Unfortunately it was conditioned on the German bishops returning their secular powers (*regalia*) to the King. True to their past form, the bishops refused to obey the Pontiff in this matter,[26] valuing their secular power more than the good of the Church.

Thus if the *status quo* of the Concordat of Worms had been the climax of the Gregorian Reform, the German bishops were the clerics on whom the Popes would have had to depend. Yet it is evident that they were undependable. Therefore further action was demanded if the clergy was to be improved. The course taken by the Popes, the only practical course open, was papal provisions.

ARTICLE 4. EVOLUTION OF PAPAL PROVISIONS

In the preliminary discussion of this thesis passing notice was taken of the existence of four types of papal provisions. The purpose of that reference was the orientation of the reader's mind for the definition of the reservation. In this present article a scientific investigation of the twelfth century will be made to determine the exact position of the reservation of the benefice in this general system of papal provisions.

The earliest recorded instance of a papal provision occurred in 1137, just fifteen years after the Concordat of Worms.[27] In a letter which Innocent II (1130-1143) addressed to Didacus the Archbishop of Compostella, the Pope counseled that a benefice be conferred on the cleric Arias. In the text of the letter the word "*mandando*" is found. It is disputed whether or not that is an interpolation.[28] Yet all are in accord that in this letter the

[26] Funk, *A manual of Church history* (2 vols., translated from the German by Perciballi and edited by Kent, London: Oates and Washbourne, Ltd., 1931), I, 343.

[27] Philippus Jaffe, *Regesta Pontificum ab condita Ecclesia ad annum post Christum natum MCXCVIII* (2nd ed. cura Wattenbach, Loewenfeld, Kaltenbrunner, Ewald, 2 vols. in I, Lipsiae, 1885-1888), n. 7831. Hereafter this work shall be quoted as Jaffe.

[28] Linden, *op. cit.*, pp. 3, 4.

Pontiff merely asked and counseled the archbishop in this regard. This is the general tenor of the letter as is evidenced by other words in the text, e. g., "*rogando.*" [29] This same note of counsel characterized all the letters of provisions sent by Lucius II (1144-1145).[30] The inherent weakness of this method of papal provisions is quite evident. Its efficacy depended wholly on the good will of the local bishops. If the latter wished to ignore it, the provision failed. Consequently there was need of another method.

By the time of Hadrian IV (1154-1159) a new type of papal provision, the mandate, was quite common.[31] It carried much more force than the counsel. Yet it was still replete with the same fundamental fault of the former. It gave the Pope's candidate no right to the benefice. That was the fundamental weakness which still had to be remedied.

In the next stage of this development of provisions a temporary solution was reached. The Popes sometimes learned of the vacancies of benefices before the local Ordinaries. In such cases it is apparent that it was not long until the Popes were conferring these benefices with the first such provision occurring during the reign of Celestine III (1191-1198).[32] This form of papal provision was known as the *ius concursus*. The Pope did not withdraw the bishop's power over the benefice but simply conferred it before the bishop did. Canonically this was a strong type of provision. Practically, however, it was extremely limited. After all, the Popes seldom knew of the vacancies before

[29] Linden, *loc. cit.*; Mollat, *La collation des benefices ecclesiastiques sous les Papes d'Avignon*, p. 42: "Les termes n'ont pas un caractere comminatoire."

[30] Linden, *op. cit.*, p. 4: "Die von beiden Päpsten gebrauchten Ausdrücke haben keinen komminatorischen Charakter."

[31] Jaffe, nn. 10,516 and 10,522: "...praecipiendo per apostolica scripta mandamus et mandando praecipimus..."

[32] *Potthast*, n. 117: "*Confirmationis nostrae manum.*"

the local bishops. The one general exception obtained when the beneficiary died in Rome.[33]

The final development of papal provisions, the reservation, removed practically all the weaknesses of the first three forms. From the legal standpoint it was almost perfect. If any inferior collator attempted to confer a reserved benefice, as a general rule he acted invalidly. The reservation of the benefice by a Roman Pontiff made its initial appearance in the year 1199 during the reign of Innocent III (1198-1216).[34]

In all, the relatively short period of sixty-two years was all that was required for the evolution of papal provisions. The climax of this development, the reservation, was reached because of the legal and practical inadequacy of the other forms.

ARTICLE 5. THE COMPLAINTS AGAINST PAPAL PROVISIONS

Before many years had passed, the system of papal provisions assumed extensive proportions. Even as early as the reign of Innocent IV (1243-1254) the papal registers record more than a thousand provisions.[35] During the Avignon period it seems probable that there were thousands of these papal provisions annually.[36] Accompanying this revolutionary change in the ecclesiastical policy was a score of complaints from every side. In view of this multitude of critics it is evident that any detailed account of individual complaints is out of the question. Instead the three most influential of the particular complaints (French Gravamina, Matthew Paris, and Bishop Grosseteste) will be treated along with the general complaint which was common to most of the critics (The Roman Curia conferred the benefices on those who offered the most money).

33 For a detailed treatment of the *ius concursus* consult Lotterius, *De re beneficiaria* (nova ed., 3 vols. in 1, Patavii, 1700), lib. II, q. XXIII.

34 *Potthast*, n. 677.

35 Linden, *op. cit.*, p. 38.

36 Cf. Barraclough, *Papal provisions*, p. 31, where he mentions that in the first three months of the reign of Clement VI (1342-1352) over 80,000 sought the Pope's good graces in this regard.

a. *French Gravamina*

The most fundamental attack against the system of papal provisions is contained in the *Gravamina Ecclesiae Gallicanae* (1247), usually called the Protestation of St. Louis (d. 1270).[37] It commences with the pathetic though amusing assertion (perhaps connected with the heretical movement of the time) that the Church has no right to possess worldly goods. This was based on the fact that Christ sent His disciples "sine argento, sine pecunia, sine virga."[38] Once this short introduction was completed, however, no time was lost in expounding their real complaint. The subject was approached from both sides, i. e., who should and who should not confer the French benefices.

For the positive consideration it was stated that the French King and his nobles possessed this right. One quotation reads: ". . . et non est multum temporis quod reges Franciae conferebant omnes episcopatus in camera sua quibus [voluerunt] . . ."[39] Even more reproachful was the accusation, "Et in hoc etiam praeiudicatur domino regi et omnibus nobilibus regni quorum filii et amici solebant promoveri spiritualibus et temporalibus incrementis."[40]

The major portion of the Gravamina is devoted to the negative consideration, namely, that the Pope should not confer French benefices. The complaint hurled at the papacy again and again is, ". . . quod nova facitis super terram; vere nova et hactenus inaudita . . . nec litera nec historia docet quod taliter fuerunt usque modo . . ."[41] To a canonist or theologian that argument proves nothing. Of the many outstanding theologians and canonists who graced the thirteenth century, not one raised

[37] Matthaeus Parisiensis, *Chronica maiora* (ed. by H. R. Lauard, Rolls Series, 7 vols., London, 1872-1883), VI, 99-112.

[38] Matthaeus Parisiensis, *ibid.*, p. 101.

[39] Matthaeus Parisiensis, *ibid.*, p. 111.

[40] *Ibid.*, p. 105.

[41] *Ibid.*, p. 100. Cf. also pp. 103, 104.

a similar complaint.[42] The papal provision of a benefice was exercised in virtue of the *plenaria amplitudo potestatis* of the papacy. In no way was it dependent on similar acts of previous Pontiffs.[43]

But what is more important is not what the statement, " quod nova facitis," proved but what it meant. It was the human side which was important in the *Gravamina.* The French had in mind the fact that for many centuries the kings and powerful laity had exercised control of the benefices. Now, if the Popes had permitted this practice for so many years, why was it not allowed to continue? Why were they to be deprived of that which was traditionally theirs? That was the fundamental cry of the *Gravamina.* That represents the attitude of the French Kings and nobles. It was a strong attitude, too, one which bred much bitterness and resistance.

b. *Chronicle of Matthew of Paris (1200-1259)*

Matthew of Paris has contributed the greatest influence to the general evaluation of papal provisions.[44] As an historian he has been of appreciable value on many points. He is not, however, always trustworthy. Consequently each statement of his must be considered carefully. Scattered throughout his work are many disparagements of papal provisions. The culmination of these attacks is reached in two sections of his *Chronicle,* in which he complains both of the depravity of the Roman Curia and of the number of foreign providees in England, and then adds that the foreign clerics beneficed by Innocent IV alone were receiving some 70,000 marks annually, just three times as much as the royal income.[45] Because that statement is mathematically so absurd, all trust must be withdrawn from Matthew's criticism of papal

[42] Wernz-Vidal, *Ius canonicum,* II, 246.

[43] Consult article 2 of Chapter VIII.

[44] Smith, *Church and state in the Middle Ages* (Oxford, Clarendon Press, 1913), p. 169.

[45] Matthaeus Parisiensis, *Chronica maiora,* IV, 419 and V, 355.

provisions. Even in the eighteenth century there was a grave suspicion that this calculation was drawn from Matthew's imagination.[46] Today that suspicion has been replaced with the certainty that this complaint was nothing more than a gross exaggeration.[47]

c. *Robert Grosseteste (c. 1175-1253)*

Robert Grosseteste, Bishop of Lincoln, (1235-1253), was one of the outstanding clerics of the Middle Ages. He was a man of humble birth, educated in France and universally recognized as a learned theologian.[48] He was the most trusted friend of and the most zealous worker for the papacy in its struggle against the English Crown.[49]

Despite this background most of the critics of papal provisions regarded and claimed Grosseteste as a fellow critic. The basis for this kinship is a letter which Matthew of Paris ascribed to the saintly bishop.[50] Luard points out the tragedy that so many men have based his character on this one letter and have classified him as anti-papal.[51]

Smith has ably demonstrated that the internal evidence of this letter proves that Grosseteste was not its author.[52] From the external evidence, that is, from the letters of Grosseteste as collected by Luard, this denial is equally patent. The letters of the

46 Thomassinus, *Vetus et nova Ecclesiae disciplina*, pars II, lib. I, c. 43, n. 9: "Quamquam ubique vehementer suspecta sit huius Historici maledicentia..."

47 Barraclough, *Papal provisions*, p. 11; Smith, *Church and state in the Middle Ages*, p. 129.

48 For his life consult *Roberti Grosseteste Episcopi quondam Lincolniensis Epistolae* edited by H. Luard (London, 1861), pp. i-xliii.

49 *Political history of England*, edited by W. Hunt and R. Poole (12 vols., London, 1906-1907), vol. III by T. Tout, 59, 90.

50 *Chronica maiora*, V, 389-392.

51 *Roberti Grosseteste epistolae*, pp. xi-xiv.

52 Smith, *op. cit.*, pp. 103, 110.

Bishop of Lincoln express nothing but love and respect for the Popes.[53] Writing to the Cardinal Legate Otto he stated: "Scio et veraciter scio domini papae et sanctae Romanae ecclesiae hanc esse potestatem ut de omnibus beneficiis ecclesiasticus libere possit ordinare." [54]

But though Grosseteste did not pen the bitter attack on the papacy, which Matthew of Paris claimed he did, nevertheless, he did complain to the Popes about some of their provisions. That is important for this study. Grosseteste was a holy man, a reformer. Furthermore he was English and yet not anti-papal. Consequently he was in a position to formulate an accurate opinion of papal provisions.

Grosseteste complained that the Pope was conferring benefices on many men who were incompetent and unsuitable.[55] There is no truth in the statement that he resented the foreign birth of the papal provides.[56] He objected that too often the papal provisions were in favor of clerics who were uneducated and too young. That is accurate and open testimony that the system of papal provisions was far from perfect. In this early period when the system was far from mature, it was not a difficult matter for a candidate to deceive the Roman Curia regarding his fitness for a benefice. It should be noted, however, that the Popes took steps to eradicate this fault as far as possible. And "from approximately the days of Innocent IV (1243-1254) onwards, the system of papal provisions was organized as a rigid, balanced, self-operative system of law, in which no room was left for papal caprice and very little for legitimate papal discretion." [57]

[53] E. g., *Epistola CXIX*, p. 340 and *Epistola XXXV*, p. 123.

[54] *Epistola XLIX*, p. 145.

[55] Luard, *Roberti Grosseteste epistolae*, nn. XVII, XIX, XLIX, LII, etc.

[56] Barraclough, *Papal provisions*, p. 13.

[57] Barraclough, *Papal provisions*, p. 90.

d. *General Complaint*

The cry, "Ecclesia Romana non supplicantium sed dantium preces exaudit," was heard from every chronicler from the fourteenth century onwards. It embodies the most serious objection against papal provisions. It was not, however, aimed at the start of papal provisions, that is, during the twelfth and thirteenth centuries. Yet on its truth or falsity depends the real worth of the mature system of papal provisions.

At the present time it is impossible to obtain a reliable judgment on the objective value of this complaint. Was the Roman Curia of the fourteenth, fifteenth and sixteenth centuries as totally debased as the chroniclers picture it? No one denies that there were excesses committed in the provision of reserved benefices. The important question is whether such abuses were prevalent and if so, to what extent. It will require years of research into the papal archives as well as the archives of local churches before any authoritative response can be given to this question. In the mean time the question stands in the balance.[58]

[58] For the bibliography on this point consult Sägmuller, *Lehrbuch des katholischen Kirchenrechts* (4th ed., Vol. I, 4 fascicles, Freiburg Br., 1925-1934), part 4, p. 571, n. 1.

CHAPTER III

The First Reservation

ARTICLE 1. THE FIRST PARTICULAR RESERVATION

It has been previously stated that the first reservation of a benefice appeared in the year 1199. This reservation was classified by most authors as a particular reservation, i. e., one which affected either one particular benefice or the benefices of one individual.[1] This classification stood in contradistinction to the general reservation. The latter was one which affected all benefices of a certain type, e. g., all those held by members of the Pope's household, all the benefices in a definite city.

That this reservation, issued on April 28, 1199,[2] was the first particular reservation is the accepted view of modern writers.[3] In his letter Innocent III notified Hugh, the Bishop of Orleans, that the first prebend to become vacant was to be reserved for the poor subdeacon, D. de Corbolio. The wording of the letter clearly stamps it as a particular reservation: ". . . quam primo vacare contigerit, nostrae donationi praecipimus reservari, personae idoneae conferendam; de qua si quid a te fuerit ordinatum, decernimus non tenere."[4] In this instance the Pope withdrew the Ordinary's power over a particular benefice, so that he could not validly confer it.

During the next few decades the Pontiffs made frequent use of the particular reservation.[5] Yet they have been assigned an

[1] Lotterius, *Tractatus de re beneficiaria*, lib. II, q. XXVI, n. 25. Here the particular reservation is defined in the sense accepted by the majority of the authors. The other connotation mentioned by Lotterius is obsolete.

[2] *Potthast*, n. 677.

[3] Linden, *op. cit.*, p. 15; Mollat, *La collation des benefices ecclésiastiques*, p. 42.

[4] *MPL*, CCXIV, 589.

[5] For some examples consult the title *De concessione ecclesiae vel praebendae non vacantis* in the *Liber Sextus*.

insignificant part in the system of reserved benefices.[6] To a great extent that estimate is justified. The particular reservation was an awkward act of administration. Each one required a separate papal bull. Nevertheless under ordinary circumstances each particular reservation reserved but one benefice. Thus even the cumulative effect of particular reservations was rather imperceptible in relation to the vast number of reserved benefices. What importance they have merited comes not from their immediate effect, but rather from the fact that they paved the way for the general reservation.

ARTICLE 2. THE FIRST GENERAL RESERVATION

One feature which must impress even the most casual student of reserved benefices is the basic importance of the decree *Licet ecclesiarum.*[7] This document was issued by Clement IV (1265-1268) on the twenty-seventh of August, 1265. The decree itself was carefully worded. In fact, its brevity is the thing which first impresses the reader. Yet for all its conciseness Pope Clement, as the glossator Ioannes Andreae remarks, expressed three distinct thoughts.

In his introductory remarks the Pope made the statement that the plenary disposition of all ecclesiastical benefices whether vacant or not belonged to the Roman Pontiff. That statement was not original with Clement. It had been the frequent and explicit enunciation of several of his predecessors. It had even found expression as early as the year 1198 when Innocent III prefaced one of his letters of papal provisions with the notice that he could so act in virtue of the "plentitudo potestatis nobis concessa."[8]

The second section of the *Licet ecclesiarum* draws attention to an ancient custom whereby the conferring of all benefices which

[6] Mollat, *La collation des benefices ecclesiastiques,* p. 23.

[7] C. 2, *De praebendis et dignitatibus,* III, 4, in VI°. For a full account of this decree see Linden, *op. cit.,* pp. 43-61.

[8] *Potthast,* n. 83; *MPL,* CCXIV, 77.

became vacant at the Apostolic See was reserved to the Roman Pontiff—". . . collationem . . . beneficiorum apud Sedem Apostolicam vacantium, specialius ceteris antiqua consuetudo Romanis Pontificibus reservavit." Many commentators regarded this portion as the most important part of the decree. They conceived this as postulating a customary law which reserved benefices before the *Licet ecclesiarum* was issued.[9] They deduced this conclusion from the explicit wording employed by Clement, " reservavit." At first that seems to be a valid inference. It must be remembered, however, that in speaking of reserved benefices the year 1265 is very early. Now in the early ages of many systems words which acquire a technical meaning with the passing of time are often used in a wide sense. That is the real problem which must be settled here. None of the standard authors have attempted to solve this point, taking it for granted. Yet there is nothing definite in the *Licet ecclesiarum* to justify this procedure. And it was in the same century that Innocent III (1198-1216) used the same word *" reservavit "* in a much wider sense than the technical meaning of reservation.[10]

Two arguments will be adduced to prove that prior to the *Licet ecclesiarum* of 1265 there was not in existence any custom regarding the reservation of benefices which became vacant *apud Sedem Apostolicam.* The first is an indirect argument which is based on the writings of the glossators. The second is a direct argument which is based on the papal registers.

Both Gulielmus Durantis (d. 1296) and Ioannes Andreae (d. 1348) are capable witnesses regarding the reason for the issuance of the *Licet ecclesiarum,* especially the former who for more than twenty years during the latter half of the thirteenth century held many positions in the Roman Curia.[11] Commenting on the

[9] Barraclough, *Papal provisions,* p. 155; Riganti, *op. cit.,* Ad regul. I, sectio I, n. 4.

[10] For several such examples consult *Potthast,* n. 3469 and *MPL,* CCXV, 22.

[11] Cicognani, *Canon Law,* authorized English version by O'Hara and Brennan (2nd ed., Philadelphia: Dolphin Press, 1935), p. 334.

Statutum of Gregory X in 1274, which modified the preceding *Licet ecclesiarum*,[12] Durantis made the following observation concerning the *Licet ecclesiarum*: "Non ergo per procuratores in curia existentes et nota quod ante constitutionem Clementis (i. e., the *Licet ecclesiarum*) prelati habebant suos procuratores in curia qui quam cito contingebat vacare aliquod beneficium ad eorum collationem spectans, illud conferebant et saepe dominum papam in conferendo praeveniebant et sibi illudebant propter quod ipse dominus Clemens motus fuit ad promulgandam illam Licet . . ." [13] The same reason was advanced by Ioannes Andreae.[14] Both of these testimonies infer that the ancient custom mentioned by Clement IV did not technically reserve benefices but rather that the Popes conferred such benefices in virtue of the *ius concursus*. This is evident from the fact that these glossators assert that the ordinary collators still had the power of conferring the benefices vacant *apud Sedem Apostolicam* in common with the Popes: ". . . saepe dominum papam in conferendo praeveniebant." Such a concept is entirely alien to the reservation which implies the withdrawal of the benefice from the power of the ordinary collator.

The second proof that this custom did not reserve benefices is garnered from the papal registers of the Popes who were the immediate predecessors of Clement IV. Linden's research in these registers was quite fruitful.[15] In all he discovered some thirty examples of papal provisions of benefices vacant *apud Sedem Apostolicam.* Now if the Popes had reserved the vast majority of these benefices, say twenty-five or more, this would indeed offer a strong contention for the existence of an ancient custom really reserving these benefices to the Pope. Yet in all these

[12] C. 3, *De praebendis et dignitatibus*, III, 4, in VI°.

[13] Quotation by E. Göller, "Zur Geschichte des zweiten Lyoner Konzils und des *Liber Sextus*"—*Römische Quartalschrift*, XX (1906), 84, 85.

[14] *Glossa ordinaria* ad c. 3, *De praebendis et dignitatibus*, III, 4, VI°, ad verba "per seipsos."

[15] Linden, *op. cit.*, pp. 31-44.

thirty cases, Linden found but one wherein the Pope had reserved the benefice in the canonical sense of the word. Furthermore, that occurred during the reign of Urban IV, who was the immediate predecessor of Clement IV, and consequently could give no foundation for an ancient custom.[16] In all the other letters there was no mention whatever of any reservation.[17]

All this evidence points directly to the conclusion that there was no ancient custom reserving these benefices to the Popes. Clement IV used the word "reservavit" in a wide sense. He meant that his predecessors had *de facto* been accustomed to confer these benefices by their *ius concursus*. Then some collators tried to void the exercise of this papal right.

The third and final section of the *Licet ecclesiarum* shows Clement lending his strong approval to the ancient custom he had just mentioned. He continued by stating most emphatically that it was his desire that this custom should be meticulously observed in the future. To insure the fulfillment of this desire he declared that if anyone conferred a benefice against this present decretal, he conferred it invalidly, "irritum ac inane." This final section represents the most important part of the decree. Its treatment here will be confined to three considerations. First an attempt will be made to determine whether major benefices which became vacant at Rome were included under this reservation. This will be followed by an explanation of the exact meaning of the phrase "*vacans apud Sedem Apostolicam.*" As a complement to these two canonical aspects, a few thoughts will be directed on the importance of the *Licet ecclesiarum* as the first general reservation.

The *Licet ecclesiarum* stated that it reserved all benefices which became vacant *apud Sedem Apostolicam*. If the wording alone is taken into account, it would seem to include all benefices, whether major or minor. Even among the minor benefices, however, there were many which escaped this reservation, e. g., man-

16 *Registres d'Urbain IV* published by L. Auvray (Paris, 1896-1910), n. 1660.

17 Linden, *op. cit.*, p. 42.

ual benefices and benefices subject to the right of lay patronage. A special section of this work will be devoted to the consideration of the exemptions among the minor benefices. Here attention is focused simply on the major benefices, i. e., abbeys, bishoprics, archbishoprics, and metropolitan sees.

The canonists under the leadership of Hostiensis (d. 1271)[18] and Ioannes Andreae (d. 1348)[19] have always taught that bishoprics and higher major offices were not included under the *Licet ecclesiarum.* Concerning the exemption of abbacies, however, they have been about equally divided in their opinions.[20]

In recent times a letter has been found in the papal registers which thoroughly justifies the canonical exemption of bishoprics and abbacies from the reservations. On June 11, 1266, Clement IV wrote to the monastery at Blagny-sur-Ternoise that his decree, the *Licet ecclesiarum,* reserved neither bishoprics nor abbacies.[21]

The meaning of Clement's phrase, "*vacans apud Sedem Apostolicam,*" has been the subject of much discussion. The expression itself is rather vague. One thing is certain—it included those minor benefices whose incumbents *died* at Rome. The seemingly unanimous opinion of the canonists maintained that the *Licet ecclesiarum* reserved these and these alone.[22] Thus it

[18] *Commentaria in quinque decretalium libros* (5 vols. in 3, Venetiis, 1581), lib. III, tit. VIII, c. 12, n. 2: "...licet aliquod ius super ecclesiis et ministris...ecclesiae promulgetur, non tamen extenditur ad episcopatus nisi ibidem de ipsis expressa ac specialis mentio habeatur."

[19] *Glossa ordinaria* ad c. 2, *De praebendis et dignitatibus,* III, 4, in VI°, ad verbum "dignitatum" where speaking of cathedral churches he asserts, "...ea quae speciali nota sunt digna, nisi specialiter notentur, neglecta intelliguntur."

[20] Garcia, *Tractatus de beneficiis* (Coloniae Allobrogum, 1636), pars V, c. I, nn. 113, 114.

[21] *Registres de Clement IV,* published by E. Jordan (Paris, 1893-1912), 319. Cf. also 706.

[22] For the list of authorities who shared this view consult Barbosa, *De officio et potestate episcopi* (3 parts in 1, Lugduni, 1628), pars II, p. 117, n. 22.

was generally held that Clement IV did not reserve those minor benefices which had been resigned in his hands, nor those which became vacant when he had promoted a cleric to a benefice incompatible with his former benefice, or when he had removed a beneficiary from his office. This canonical opinion was based not on the *Licet ecclesiarum* itself, but on the decretal *Praesenti* issued by Boniface VIII in 1298.[23] In this decretal Boniface clarified the issue for the future ruling that the *Licet ecclesiarum* was to reserve only those benefices whose incumbents had died at Rome. With this meager information to guide them, most canonists inferred that the same interpretation had been shared by the predecessors of Boniface.

In the light of modern historical research, however, that view is no longer admissible. Linden has ably demonstrated this conclusion by his thorough investigation of the papal registers of that period.[24] One can summarize his research by stating that between the years 1265 and 1298 the *Licet ecclesiarum* was not subject to a uniform interpretation. Several Popes gave this decretal a strict interpretation, i. e., they held that a benefice was to be considered *vacans apud Sedem Apostolicam* only when the incumbent *died* at the Holy See. The remaining Pontiffs gave this decretal a broad interpretation, i. e., they considered benefices vacant at the Holy See even when the Pope had accepted the resignation of the incumbent, or when he had removed the incumbent from the benefice.

One last consideration remains to be treated in this article, namely, to point out the importance of the *Licet ecclesiarum* as the first general reservation. Unfortunately most authors have classified this decretal not as the first general reservation, but rather as the first *written* general reservation. They have in mind the preceding customary law mentioned by Clement IV. Since this custom did not reserve benefices, the *Licet ecclesiarum* merits the unqualified title, the first general reservation.

[23] C. 34, *De praebendis et dignitatibus*, III, 4, in VI°.

[24] Linden, *op. cit.*, pp. 48-52.

There is no reason to believe that this general law of the Church reserved an immense number of benefices. This is evidenced by the really small number of benefices vacant *apud Sedem Apostolicam* mentioned in the papal registers of that time. Thus, if the direct results were the only consideration, the *Licet ecclesiarum* would not merit much importance. Its value, however, must be estimated principally from the influence it exerted on the future activity of the Popes. As Göller fittingly remarks, it deserves recognition because it was the impulse which gave rise to the immense system of reserved benefices which was so characteristic of the Middle Ages.[25]

[25] Göller, "Zur Geschichte des zweiten Lyoner Konzils und des *Liber Sextus*"—*Römische Quartalschrift,* XX (1906), 84.

CHAPTER IV

Historical Development of Reserved Benefices

ARTICLE 1. THE APPROACH TO THE STUDY OF THIS DEVELOPMENT

In the preceding chapters some consideration has been given to the definition of a reservation, to the reform motives which prompted the Pontiffs to reserve benefices, to the criticism of reservations, and finally to the first historical appearances of the particular and general reservations. There now remains the difficult task of sketching the historical and canonical growth of reserved benefices throughout the succeeding centuries.

There are two possible avenues of approach to the study of this subject. On the one hand this development could be traced in a strictly chronological order. The alternative course would be to classify the various types of reserved benefices and then trace the historical growth of each classification. At first glance the former method would seem to present a better historical approach to this subject. Yet, in view of several practical difficulties the purely chronological order will be foregone in the present discussion. First there is the uniform practice on the part of all authors to shun this method. Then there is the vastness and complexity of the reservations which would prove too cumbersome and involved for a strictly chronological digest.

Both of these factors persuade the employment of the method of first systematizing and then tracing. Another factor which motivates this same course is that the classification of reserved benefices has already been made by the competent legal authorities, i. e., by the Popes. This classification is found in the *Regulae Cancellariae.*

ARTICLE 2. THE REGULAE CANCELLARIAE

As the exercise of ecclesiastical power became more and more centralized, the work which fell to the hands of the Roman Pontiffs became increasingly involved. To facilitate the speedy transaction of this growing business the Popes issued a set of practical regulations as a guide for the Roman Curia. At first these rules were in the form of oral instructions.[1] It remained for John XXII (1316-1334) to reduce them to writing by entrusting their editing to his vice-chancellor, Cardinal Pierre le Tessier (d. 1325), and thus to supply the initial movement which was to determine their form under the succeeding Popes. It is in this sense that one must interpret the statement that the *Regulae Cancellariae* were started by John XXII.[2] The tendency of some authors to credit this same Pontiff as the founder of all the reservations of benefices in the *Regulae Cancellariae* has no historical foundation.

Reserved benefices were, of course, but one concern of the curia. Consequently not all of the rules of the *Regulae Cancellariae* dealt with reservations. Once this system was fairly well developed, there were approximately seventy-two rules. Of these the first eleven usually contained the regulations regarding the reservation of benefices.[3]

Each Pope issued his own set of *Regulae Cancellariae*. The question must be settled, then, as to which set of *Regulae Cancellariae* should be selected for this study of reserved benefices. From this wide range the set issued by Clement XI (1700-1721)

[1] Riganti, *In proemium operis*, n. 3.

[2] Ottenthal, *Regulae Cancellariae Apostolicae, Die Päpstlichen Kanzleiregeln von Johannes XXII bis Nicolaus V* (Innsbruck, 1888), p. ix; Phillips, *Kirchenrecht* (8 vols., Regensburg, 1845-1889, vol. VIII by F. Vering), IV, 489; Cicognani, *Canon Law*, pp. 322, 323.

[3] The reader is referred to Göller for a critical bibliography of the commentators of the *Regulae Cancellariae*. E. Göller, "Die Kommentatoren der päpstlichen Kanzleiregeln vom Ende des 15. bis zum Beginn des 17. Jahrhunders" — *Archiv für katholisches Kirchenrecht*, LXXXV (1905), 440-460.

has been chosen. The reason for this selection is that after the time of Clement XI there were no changes whatever in the *Regulae Cancellariae.*[4]

The plan to be followed in sketching the historical and canonical development of these reservations will be as follows. First the reservation will be stated as it was promulgated by Clement XI. Then an attempt will be made to determine the origin of this reservation and to trace any important changes in the legislation on this point. Whenever the origin of the rule is the only data presented, that will be an indication that there were no changes in this legislation under the succeeding Popes.

a. *Regula prima*

There are ten rules of the *Regulae Cancellariae* of Clement XI which contain reservations. Of these ten the first is by far the most complicated. It lays the foundation for this characteristic by basing its reservations on three distinct sources: the *Ad regimen* of Benedict XII (1334-1342) in the year 1335,[5] the *Execrabilis* of John XXII (1316-1334) in the year 1317,[6] and the Council of Trent. An analysis of the rule itself discloses that it enfolds ten distinct reservations. Of the three sources just mentioned, the latter two each contribute one reservation, the remaining eight being derived from the *Ad regimen.*

The *Ad regimen* was, of course, quite comprehensive. But as Benedict remarked in the initial sentences of this decretal, much of the content matter was a repetition of the work of his predecessors. To this Pontiff, however, belongs the credit of having merged his own enactments with those of his predecessors with accurate preciseness. So well was this task accomplished that everyone of his successors repeated the *Ad regimen* in the *Regulae Cancellariae.*[7]

[4] Van Hove, *Prolegomena* (*Commentarium Lovaniense,* vol. I, tom. I, Mechliniae et Romae: Dessain, 1928), p. 190.

[5] C. 13, *De praebendis et dignitatibus,* III, 2, in Extravag. com.

[6] C. un., *De praebendis et dignitatibus,* tit. III, in Extravag. Ioann. XXII.

[7] Riganti, In regul. I, sectio I, n. 1.

The eight classes of benefices reserved by the *Ad regimen* will be stated in the following numerical order:

1. *All patriarchal, archiepiscopal, and episcopal churches, as well as all monasteries, dignities, and all other ecclesiastical benefices with or without the care of souls, which became vacant apud Sedem Apostolicam.*

There is a striking resemblance between this reservation and that contained in the *Licet ecclesiarum.* But this resemblance is not so close as to stamp this decree as a mere repetition of Clement's enactment. A scrutiny of the laws themselves reveals two discrepancies. Other than these distinctions one must note two extraneous limitations on the original reservation of the *Licet ecclesiarum.* These four differentiations will be explained in the order of their chronological appearance.

Just nine years after the issuance of the *Licet ecclesiarum* the first modification of this decree was embodied in the *Statutum* of Gregory X (1271-1276).[8] Gregory ruled that if the Pope did not confer a benefice vacant at the Holy See within one month from the day it became vacant, the benefice was no longer reserved. Two opinions soon arose concerning the computation of the month alloted to the Pope. Guilelmus de Monte Lauduno (d. 1343) held that it was *tempus utile.* But the opinion advanced by Ioannes Andreae (d. 1348), namely, that it was *tempus continuum,*[9] was more in accord with the purpose of the law (prevention of long vacancies) and soon prevailed.[10]

A second limitation was imposed on the *Licet ecclesiarum* when Boniface VIII (1294-1303) enacted the decretal *Si Apostolica.*[11] The effect of this law was that all parochial churches and other churches with the care of souls which became vacant *apud Sedem*

[8] C. 3, *De praebendis et dignitatibus,* III, 4, in VI°.

[9] *Glossa ordinaria* ad verbum "mensem", c. 3, III, 4, in VI°: "...istud tempus non a tempore scientiae sed vacationis currere."

[10] Riganti, In regul. I, sectio I, n. 377.

[11] C. 35, *De praebendis et dignitatibus,* III, 4, in VI°.

Apostolicam while the Holy See itself was vacant were not reserved. This was occasioned by the long interregnum which had followed the death of Nicholas IV in 1292. It should be noted here that most of the reservations in the *Regulae Cancellariae* did not bind when the Holy See was vacant. The one exception was the reservation contained in the *Licet ecclesiarum* (i. e., affecting those benefices vacant *apud Sedem Apostolicam*), which had been issued as a perpetual law.

The other two differences are noticeable from the wording of the two decretals. The *Ad regimen* explicitly reserved patriarchal, archiepiscopal, and episcopal churches vacant at the Holy See. It was pointed out earlier in this work that the *Licet ecclesiarum* did not include these major benefices. Clement V (1305-1314) mentioned these for the first time in his *Etsi pastoralis* of 1305.[12]

The second note which evidences greater comprehensiveness in the *Ad regimen* is the phrase "*quomodocumque vacantia apud Sedem Apostolicam.*" Previous reference has been made to the fluctuating interpretation given to the *Licet ecclesiarum* on this matter. In 1316, however, in the *Ex debito* of John XXII an explicit reservation was placed on benefices vacant at the Holy See by means other than death, e. g., deposition, transfer.[13] Benedict included this note in the *Ad regimen.*[14]

2. *All major and minor benefices which became vacant because of a deposition, privation, or transfer made by the Apostolic authority.*

One fact which should be made clear before any further progress is made is that not all the reservations of the *Regulae Cancellariae* were mutually exclusive. This particular section, which was introduced by John XXII in the *Ex debito*, overlapped on part of the first section of the *Ad regimen.* Yet the distinction

12 C. 3, *De praebendis et dignitatibus*, III, 2. In Extravag. com.

13 C. 4, *De electione*, I, 3, in Extravag. com.

14 Cf. the text: "... quomodocumque vacantia ..."

which existed is quite noticeable. The first section of the *Ex debito* considered only those instances wherein one was deprived of his benefice while he was *apud Sedem Apostolicam*. The *Ad regimen* comprised also those cases in which the incumbent lapsed from the tenure of his benefice while absent from the Apostolic See.

3. *All benefices which were the object of an election or postulation which was declared null or in which the one who was elected or postulated renounced the same and his renunciation was accepted by the Apostolic See.*

Benedict XII borrowed this bodily from the *Ex debito.*

4. *All benefices of the cardinals and of the officials of the Holy See.*

This was another reservation adopted from the *Ex debito.* That it originated with John XXII is now doubtful. Using indirect testimony Lux has demonstrated the possibility if not the probability that this reservation existed under John's predecessor, Clement V.[15] Both John XXII and Benedict XII gave lists of the "*officiales.*" Of these two lists, neither of which is exhaustive,[16] the more complete one was presented by Benedict. It read as follows: ". . . camerarii, vicecancellarii, notarii, auditorum literarum contradictarum, et apostolici palatii causarum auditorum, correctorum et scriptorum literarum Apostolicarum, ac poenitentiarii praefatae sedis, ac abbreviatorum, necnon commensalium et aliorum quorumlibet capellanorum sedis eiusdem, et etiam quorumcumque legatorum sive nunciorum, ac in terris ecclesiae Romanae rectorum et thesauriorum per dictum Ioannem praedecessorem vel nos specialiter deputatorum . . ."

This section of the rule states explicitly that it does not affect benefices obtained by a cleric before he became an official of the Holy See. Then in 1431 Eugene IV (1431-1437) extended this

15 Lux, p. 20.

16 Riganti, In regul. I, sectio IV, nn. 269, 270.

exemption to those benefices obtained by a cleric after he had ceased to be an "*officialis.*"[17]

5. *Benefices which became vacant when the one who was approaching or leaving the Roman Curia died within two days' journey of the same.*

This reservation made its original appearance in the decree *Praesenti* of Boniface VIII in 1298.[18] The two days' journey was a technical term denoting forty milliaria (forty Italian miles).[19] Great stress was placed on the element of approaching or leaving the curia. Thus if the curia is approaching or leaving the cleric (and the curia travelled frequently in past centuries), the circumstances required for this rule would not be fulfilled.

6. *Benefices of the members of the Roman Curia who in leaving the curia died in a place which was not their domicile and at the same time was within two days' journey of the curia.*

This was also taken from the *Praesenti* of Boniface VIII.

7. *Benefices of those who were promoted to a patriarchal, archiepiscopal, or episcopal church or to an abbacy.*

This reservation of the *Ad regimen* was probably the only original contribution made by Benedict XII. The important canonical consideration was that it did not reserve the benefice of a cleric promoted to the cardinalate.

8. *Benefices which became vacant because of the incompatibility of another benefice conferred by the authority of the Apostolic See.*

This reservation was first issued by John XXII on September 15, 1316, in his decretal *Ex debito.*[20]

[17] Ottenthal, *op. cit.*, pp. 238-254, *Regulae Cancellariae Eugenii Papae IV.*

[18] C. 34, *De praebendis et dignitatibus*, III, 4, in VI°.

[19] Cf. the glossa of Ioannes Andreae on the words: "duas dietas legales."

[20] Lux, p. 25.

EXSECRABILIS

The first rule of the *Regulae Cancellariae* repeated the reservation made by John XXII in the *Exsecrabilis* (1317).[21] This law, which made its initial appearance under John XXII, reserved all benefices which were maliciously retained by one who had already possessed a benefice incompatible with them. Like so many of the rules of the *Regulae Cancellariae* this one underwent no changes under the succeeding Popes. The canonical concept of incompatibility, however, was the subject of much development.[22]

COUNCIL OF TRENT

The final section of the first rule is concerned with the Council of Trent. Though this Council passed much legislation regarding the conferring of benefices, not one reservation was enacted. It was not long, however, until its laws were made the basis for reservations. In 1567 Pius V (1566-1572) issued the Constitution *In conferendis*.[23] Its primary purpose was to reserve all benefices conferred against the form required by Trent. The essential form required by this Council was that an examination be held for the conferring of all vacant parochial benefices. From the candidates approved by the examiners the bishops were to choose the most worthy.[24] In 1590 this reservation was placed in the first rule of the *Regulae Cancellariae* by Gregory XIV (1590-1591).[25]

This form was not the only requirement of the Council of Trent which was made the basis for a reservation. There were

21 C. un., *De praebendis et dignitatibus,* tit. III, Extravag. Ioann. XXII.

22 For a detailed account confer Thomassinus, *Vetus et nova disciplina Ecclesiae,* pars II, lib. III, capita 5-9; Wernz-Vidal, *Ius canonicum,* II, nn. 214, 215.

23 *Bullarium Romanum,* VII, 555.

24 Conc. Trident., sess. XXIV, *de ref.*, c. 18.

25 *Regulae Cancellariae S. D. N. Gregorii XIV* (Romae, 1590), Regula prima.

four decrees of Trent concerning the recipient of a benefice. In 1585 Sixtus V stated in the first rule of his *Regulae Cancellariae* that all benefices conferred in violation of these decrees were reserved to the Pope.

The following is a brief summary of these decrees:

a) *Age*: No one could obtain a benefice before he had reached his fourteenth year of age.[26]

b) *Legitimacy*: A cleric born of an illegitimate marriage could not receive a benefice in the church in which his father has or had a benefice.[27]

c) *Homicide*: One who committed voluntary homicide could receive no benefice.[28]

d) *Regulars*: If a benefice belonged to regulars, it had to be conferred on a member of that particular order. Likewise, if the benefice belonged to the secular clergy, it had to be conferred on one of the seculars.[29]

b. *Regula secunda*

The study of the reservations contained in the first rule of the *Regulae Cancellariae* centered on an analysis of several documents, most of which are accessible in the *Corpus Iuris Canonici* together with any collection of the decrees of the Council of Trent. For most of the other nine rules, however, the approach to the documentary evidence is not quite so simplified for one must consult the various *Regulae Cancellariae* of the different Popes.

Since each Roman Pontiff issued a set of *Regulae Cancellariae*, this material is rather extensive. Fortunately Ottenthal in his fine work which has been previously cited has collected all the sets of the *Regulae* of the Popes from John XXII (1316-1334) to Nicholas V (1447-1455). Since most of the reservations of the

[26] Sess. XXIII, *de ref.*, c. 6. Cf. also sess. XXIV, *de ref.*, c. 12.

[27] Sess. XXV, *de ref.*, c. 15.

[28] Sess. XIV, *de ref.*, c. 7.

[29] Sess. XIV, *de ref.*, cc. 10, 11.

Regulae Cancellariae had reached the apex of their development by the time of this latter Pontiff,[30] the path is open for a clear understanding of these reservations. Furthermore with reference to those innovations which occurred in a later period a sufficient number of sets of the *Regulae* has been available to this writer to present an accurate picture of these changes.

The second rule of the *Regulae Cancellariae* reserved three types of benefices:

1. *All patriarchal, primatial, archiepiscopal, and episcopal Sees.*

For many centuries the Church has regarded the control of these major benefices as a prime requisite for the proper governing of the faithful. Assertions concerning the initial appearance of this general reservation range anywhere from Boniface VIII (1294-1303) to Urban V (1362-1370). It did not, however, become part of the Church's general legislation until August 3, 1363, when Urban V placed it in his *Regulae Cancellariae*.[31] The mistaken belief in an earlier appearance of this general reservation can be traced to the numerous particular reservations of episcopal sees by the preceding Pontiffs, so numerous indeed that their accumulative effect approached the results of a general reservation.[32]

When Urban V first issued this reservation, it affected all patriarchal, primatial, archiepiscopal, and episcopal sees. Three months later he altered the wording of the rule so that it embraced only those sees whose annual income exceeded two hundred gold florins.[33] His successor, Gregory XI (1370-1378) with-

[30] Scherer, *Handbuch des Kirchenrechtes* (2 vols., Graz-Leipzig, 1886-1898), I, 295, footnote 5.

[31] *Regulae Cancellariae Urbani Papae V*—Ottenthal, *Regulae Cancellariae Apostolicae*, p. 17, n. 18; Lux, p. 43.

[32] G. Mollat, *Jean XXII (1316-1334)*, *Lettres communes* (14 vols., Paris: Boccard, 1904-1935), vol. XIV (Index) under the words "Reservationes ecclesiarum cathedralium." This will give the reader an idea of the numerous reservations of episcopal sees made by this Pope alone.

[33] Ottenthal, *op. cit.*, p. 15, n. 6.

drew this limitation,[34] setting the example which was followed in the future.

2. *Monasteries of men which had an annual income in excess of two hundred gold florins.*

The history of this reservation has consistently paralleled the history of the reservation of episcopal sees. The reason for this similarity is to be found in the fact that they were considered equivalent to cathedral churches and thus were regarded as consistorial benefices.[35]

The original form of this rule as enacted by Urban V on August 3, 1363, reserved all monasteries both of men and of women.[36] Three months later he withdrew this reservation of monasteries of women and restricted the reservation of monasteries of men to those with an annual income in excess of one hundred gold florins.[37] But most of his successors extended the reservation only to those monasteries of men in which the annual income exceeded two hundred florins.

3. *Benefices which became vacant while the patriarchal, primatial, archiepiscopal, or episcopal see itself was vacant, or while the one who had been named to that see had not taken peaceful possession of the same.*

This reservation was incorporated in the *Regulae Cancellariae* at a comparatively late time, namely, on March 9, 1568, when Pope Pius V (1566-1572) issued the Constitution *Sanctissimus*.[38] His successor, Gregory XIII (1572-1585), was the sole Pope to omit this reservation from the *Regulae Cancellariae*.[39]

In the form in which it was issued by Pius V it reserved only those benefices which became vacant while the see itself was

34 Ottenthal, *op. cit.*, p. 28, n. 29.

35 Riganti, In regul. II, sectio II, nn. 5, 9.

36 Ottenthal, *op. cit.*, p. 17, n. 18.

37 Ottenthal, *op. cit.*, p. 15, n. 6.

38 *Bullarium Romanum*, VII, 659, n. 5.

39 Riganti, In regul. II, sectio III, n. 5.

vacant, i. e., until someone had been promoted to fill the vacancy. Gregory XIV (1590-1591) extended the rule to include those benefices which became vacant before the one who was appointed had taken peaceful possession of the see.[40]

This rule stated that it reserved only those benefices the free and unrestricted bestowal of which (*libera collatio*) belonged to the bishop. Thus, if someone had the right of presenting a candidate for a particular benefice, that benefice was not reserved by this rule.[41] The canonists made a distinction when there was question of alternate conferrings, e. g., when the bishop and the cathedral chapter took turns in conferring the benefice. If it was only the *exercise* of the right of conferring which was involved, e. g., when the right to confer a benefice was vested in a cardinal who allowed the bishop the exercise of this right, then the benefice was never reserved by this rule. If the right itself of conferring was alternated, then the benefice was reserved if it happened to be the bishop's turn to confer it.[42] It was disputed whether this second rule affected benefices in a vacant diocese in which the deceased ruler had been a cardinal.[43]

c. *Regula tertia*

The third rule of the *Regulae Cancellariae* reserved *all benefices which were resigned by anyone who had received or who was about to receive from the Pope a benefice which was incompatible with the one which had been resigned.*

It has already been explained that one of the sections of the first rule of the *Regulae Cancellariae* reserved all benefices which became vacant because of the incompatibility of another benefice

[40] *Regulae Cancellariae Apostolicae S. D. N. Gregorii Papae XIV* (Romae, 1590), regula secunda.

[41] Gonzalez, *Glossema seu commentatio ad regulam octavam cancellariae de reservatione mensium* (Romae, 1604), gloss. XXXXV, sectio III, n. 4. Hereafter this will be cited *De reservatione mensium*.

[42] Gonzalez, *ibid.*, nn. 49-51.

[43] Garcia, *Tractatus de beneficiis*, pars V, c. I, nn. 252-256.

conferred by the authority of the Apostolic See.[44] But it proved a rather easy matter to avoid this reservation. The procedure consisted simply in the cleric resigning his original benefice before accepting the papal provision proffered him. To nullify such evasions Gregory XV (1621-1623) placed this reservation in the *Regulae* he issued.[45]

d. *Regula quarta*

The fourth rule, which enfolds six types of reserved benefices, is ascribed by Riganti and others to John XXII in 1316.[46] In view of the complete lack of documentary evidence to substantiate such a contention it should be disregarded. Probably it is based on the influence of certain early writers who tended to acknowledge John XXII as the author of all the reservations in the *Regulae Cancellariae.*

The benefices reserved therein were the following:

1. *That dignity which was considered the major one after the episcopal dignity in every cathedral, metropolitan, or patriarchal church.*

In most cathedral churches several clerics were the recipients of privileges of preeminence and added jurisdiction, e. g., provosts, deans, etc. This reservation was concerned only with the one dignity which had received the greatest privileges in this line.[47] It made its first appearance in the *Regulae Cancellariae* of the anti-Pope Benedict XIII (1394-1417).[48] This reservation was utilized by the true Pontiffs with an occasional limitation to those dignities with an annual income in excess of ten gold florins.[49]

[44] *Supra,* p. 36.

[45] D. Roderico de Quesada y Molina, *Notae seu indices breves ad Regulas Cancellariae Apostolicae S. D. N. Gregorii XV* (Romae, 1622), pp. 24, 25.

[46] Riganti, In regul. IV, sectio I, n. 3.

[47] Garcia, *Tractatus de beneficiis,* pars V, c. I, nn. 262-264.

[48] *Regulae Cancellariae Benedicti Papae XIII*—Ottenthal, *op. cit.,* p. 124, n. 2.

[49] *Regulae Cancellariae Alexandri Papae VIII* (Romae, 1689), p. 11; *Regulae Cancellariae Benedicti Papae XIII* (Romae, 1724), p. 11.

2. *The principal dignity in a collegiate church which (dignity) had an annual income in excess of ten gold florins.*

This reservation also originated with the anti-Pope Benedict XIII.[50] The only variation noticeable in this rule was that some of the Popes reserved these same dignities even when their income was less than ten gold florins.

3. *Priories, conventual dignities of regulars, and prelatial superintendencies (praepositurae).*

4. *The tenures of preceptories general (praeceptoriae generales) in any order other than a military order.*

5. *Benefices of the members of the Pope's household.*

Etymologically a member of the Pope's household is anyone who renders personal service to the Pope and in return receives either sustenance or a salary.[51] It will be found that relatively few individuals meet both these requisites. As time progressed, however, the term "*familiaris*" assumed a meaning broader than its natural connotation. By positive enactments the Popes extended the ambit of this term so that it included various officials of the Holy See as well as other clerics. Successive decrees of the Pontiffs enumerated the following as *familiares Pontificis*: "Cubicularii, scutiferi, militares S. Petri et Pauli, conclavistae et alii officiales ex palatio panem habentes, auditores Rotae, secretarii, scriptores litterarum apostolicarum, prothonotarii non participantes in pane apostolica, cantores capellae pontificae, scriptores in Bibliotheca Vaticana, et notarius S. Poenitentiariae."[52]

The first one to reserve the benefices of the members of the papal household was Urban VI (1378-1389).[53] Eugene IV (1431-1447) restricted this rule to those benefices obtained while

[50] Ottenthal, *op. cit.*, p. 124, n. 2.

[51] Lotterius, *De re beneficiaria*, lib. II, q. XXXIII, n. 18; Riganti, In regul. IV, sectio V, nn. 76, 96.

[52] H. Gonzalez, *De reservatione mensium*, gloss. LI, nn. 20, sq.

[53] *Regulae Cancellariae Urbani Papae VI*—Ottenthal, *op. cit.*, p. 53, n. 29.

one was a member of the papal household.[54] Almost all the other Popes, however, also reserved those benefices acquired before the cleric became a member of the household.[55] This rule never affected those benefices obtained by a cleric after he had lost this honor of membership in the papal household.

6. *Benefices of the members of the cardinal's household.*

This reservation was originally placed in the *Regulae Cancellariae* by the anti-Pope Clement VII (1378-1394).[56] It was subject to the same interpretation as the preceding section of this rule with this one exception, that the benefice was not reserved until the cleric had been a member of the cardinal's household for four successive months. This limitation is deduced from rule thirty-two of the *Regulae,* which contains the instructions for those applying for this type of reserved benefice.[57]

e. *Regula quinta*

The fifth rule reserved those *benefices which the collectors of the Apostolic Camera had obtained during their office as collectors as well as the corresponding benefices of any subcollector who was the only one to have this duty in a given diocese.*

Even before this rule was promulgated some considered these collectors and subcollectors to be officials of the Holy See and maintained that their benefices were reserved on this score.[58] Pope Urban V (1362-1370) removed any doubts concerning their reservation when he placed this rule in the *Regulae Cancellariae* on June 30, 1363.[59] The sole variation in this reservation is wit-

[54] *Regulae Cancellariae Eugenii Papae IV*—Ottenthal, *op. cit.*, p. 239, n. 3.

[55] Lotterius, *op. cit.*, lib. II, q. XXXII, n. 76.

[56] *Regulae Cancellariae Clementis Papae VII*—Ottenthal, *op. cit.*, p. 113, n. 102.

[57] *Regulae Cancellariae Clementis Papae XI*—Reiffenstuel, *Ius canonicum universum,* lib. III, tit. V, n. 487: "...qui ipsorum cardinalium familiares continui commensales ad minus per quattuor menses..."

[58] Riganti, In regul. V, n. 186.

[59] *Regulae Cancellariae Urbani Papae V*—Ottenthal, *op. cit.*, p. 15, n. 5.

nessed in the renewal by Gregory XI in 1370. He did not reserve the benefices of subcollectors.[60]

f. *Regula sexta*

The sixth rule reserved the *benefices of members of the Roman Curia who died while following the curia from place to place.* Its origin can be traced to Urban V who placed it in the *Regulae* on December 17, 1367.[61] A few canonists have confused this reservation with the *Ad regimen*, which reserved the benefices of one who while approaching or leaving the curia died within two days' journey of the same. That, however, is a mistake. There is an evident distinction between these two reservations.

g. *Regula septima*

The seventh rule reserved the *benefices of the papal chamberlains (cubicularii) and the papal couriers (cursores)*. To a great extent this rule overlapped the reservation of the benefices of the officials of the Pope as well as the reservation of the benefices of the members of his household. It was admitted that most of the chamberlains enjoyed one or both of these honors. There was a question raised, however, whether a certain few enjoyed either of these privileges.[62] It is the benefices of these chamberlains and couriers which are reserved by the seventh rule.

The reservation of the benefices of the papal chamberlains was incorporated in the *Regulae Cancellariae* of the anti-Pope Innocent VII (1404-1406).[63] The papal couriers first received explicit mention under Pope Nicholas V (1447-1455).[64] The only major change in this rule was the inclusion of the reservation of the benefices of honorary chamberlains, Gregory XV (1621-1623) placing this in the *Regulae*.[65]

[60] *Regulae Cancellariae Gregorii Papae XI*—Ottenthal, p. 28, n. 15.

[61] Ottenthal, *op. cit.*, p. 23, n. 38.

[62] Lotterius, *De re beneficiaria*, lib. II, q. XXXII, n. 162; Riganti, In regul. VII, n. 23.

[63] Ottenthal, *op. cit.*, p. 83, n. 2.

[64] Ottenthal, *Regulae Cancellariae Apostolicae*, p. 256, n. 6.

[65] Quesada y Molina, *Notae ad Regulas Cancellariae Gregorii XV*, p. 38.

h. *Regula octava*

The eighth rule contained two reservations:

1. *Benefices in the churches of St. Peter, St. John Lateran, and St. Mary Major.*

This section of the rule originated with Pope Martin V (1417-1431).[66] There was no historical or canonical development of this reservation. There is, however, the perennial question: Why did the Pope reserve these benefices? After all he was the only Ordinary for the city of Rome. The answer is that the right of conferring some of these benefices had been granted to various archbishops.[67]

2. *Benefices in the titular churches of cardinals who were absent from the Roman Curia.*

This reservation was first enacted by Pope Nicholas V (1447-1455).[68] Alexander VII (1655-1667) changed this law so that it did not reserve the benefices of a cardinal who was absent from the curia either because he was residing in his own church or because he was doing work for the Holy See[69] but he was the only one to so legislate.

The Council of Trent insisted that the cardinals who were Ordinaries outside of Rome reside personally in their dioceses.[70] If the cardinals obeyed the mandate of the Council, it seems naturally to follow that they lost the right to confer the benefices in their titular churches. The best solution to this difficulty is the practical consideration advanced by Garcia, namely, that as a matter of fact the Popes granted to the cardinals the right to confer these benefices.[71]

66 Quesada, *Notae ad Regulas Cancellariae Gregorii XV*, p. 38.

67 Gonzalez, *De reservatione mensium*, gloss. XIII, n. 21.

68 Ottenthal, *op. cit.*, p. 256, n. 7.

69 *Regulae Cancellariae S. D. N. Alexandri VII* (Romae, 1655), p. 18.

70 Sess. 23, *de ref.*, c. 1.

71 *Tractatus de beneficiis*, pars V, cap. I, n. 406.

i. *Regula nona*

The ninth rule is composed of two sections, the first containing a reservation and the second the privilege of conferring some of the benefices reserved in the first section.

1. The reservation, which is termed the *regula mensium*, affected all ecclesiastical *benefices which became vacant during the months of January, February, April, May, July, August, October, and November in any manner other than by resignation.* It is the most extensive of all the reservations. Though it was first issued by Nicholas V in 1447,[72] it was not introduced into the *Regulae Cancellariae* until some time later. The date of this incorporation in the *Regulae* is rather obscure. Certainly it was contained in the *Regulae* of Pope Gregory XIV (1590-1591).[73] Though some authorities state that this was its first appearance in the *Regulae,* one can accept the testimony of Gonzalez that it was in the *Regulae* of Pope Pius V (1566-1572), being numbered as rule sixty-nine.[74]

2. The privilege which was granted to patriarchs, archbishops, and bishops who resided in their dioceses was the right to confer the benefices which became vacant during the months of February, April, June, August, October, and December and which were not reserved by any other rule. This is known as the privilege of the alternate months. Its primary effect was to reduce the number of months reserved to the Pope from eight to six.

Though the *regula mensium* had appeared as early as 1447, there is no notice of the accompanying privilege before the reign of Paul II (1464-1467). Even at this time only a few concessions were granted to individual bishops.[75] Though such favors

[72] Hinschius, *Kirchenrecht,* III, 153; Riganti, In regul. IX, proemium, n. 2.

[73] *Regulae Cancellariae S. D. N. Gregorii Papae XIV* (Romae, 1590), regula nona.

[74] Gonzalez, *De reservatione mensium,* gloss. I, n. 6.

[75] Riganti, In regul. IX, proemium, n. 8.

were granted with increasing frequency, it was not until the year 1514 that this privilege was extended by Pope Leo X (1513-1521) and made available for all the bishops.[76]

j. *Regula undecima*

The eleventh rule (the tenth contains no reservation) states that all bishoprics, monasteries, and other ecclesiastical benefices which the preceding Popes had reserved were to remain reserved even if they became vacant after the death of the Pope. Strictly considered this is not a reservation, but rather an explanation of the permanency of the reservation. The thought expressed by this rule may be illustrated by the following example. Let it be supposed that the Pope had made a certain pastor a member of the papal household on July 1. Now, if the Pope died on July 5 and the pastor on July 6, was the latter's benefice reserved to the next Pope? The answer, as the eleventh rule indicated, was in the affirmative. Some earlier canonists attempted to deny the reservation of such a benefice by arguing that the *Regulae Cancellariae* did not bind during the vacancy of the Holy See. That argument, however, was irrelevant. Canonically, the benefice in question became reserved on July 1, when the pastor was made a member of the papal household.

The rule itself made its initial appearance in the *Regulae Cancellariae* during the reign of Paul II (1464-1471).[77] The only change under the succeeding Popes was the gradual transformation into a more legal and technical wording.

[76] Lotterius, *op. cit.*, lib. II, q. XXXVII, n. 11; Rigant, *ibid.*, n. 10.

[77] C. 14, III, 2, In Extravag. com.

CHAPTER V

Penal Reservations

The Regulae Cancellariae proved the most fruitful but not the only source of reserved benefices. Scattered over the thirteenth and the following centuries are numerous papal letters and constitutions containing general reservations. The copiousness of such documents tends to exaggerate what importance they possessed. This same diffusiveness renders the systematic treatment of these miscellaneous reservations quite difficult. In this chapter only the penal reservations will be mentioned. Thus the non-penal reservations will be ignored, e. g., at times the early Popes reserved the benefices in the diocese which they ruled before they were elected to the papacy. Since this type of general reservation occurred so infrequently, to ignore it will be to detract very little from this study of reserved benefices.

A penal reservation may be described as one whereby the Pope reserves the benefices of those who have committed a definite crime. The various crimes form the basis for the following division of this type of reservation.

1. *Political crimes*—This form of reservation characterized only the most ancient period of reserved benefices. It was aimed primarily at those clerics who supported the German Kings in their battles with the Popes, especially on the question of the Papal States. Lux gives several examples of these general reservations during the reign of Clement IV.[1]

2. *Heresy*—After the time of Luther many clerics defected from the faith. In 1559 Pope Paul IV declared that such clerics were automatically deprived of their benefices.[2] Eight years

[1] Lux, pp. 16, 17.

[2] Const. *Cum ex apostolatus*, 15 febr. 1559, § 5—*Codicis iuris canonici fontes cura Emi. Petri Card. Gasparri editi* (9 vols., Romae: Typis Poly-

later Pope Pius V ruled that such benefices were reserved.[3]

3. *Simony*—This delinquency, which has given the Church so much trouble, finally furnished the basis for a reservation under Pope Pius IV (1559-1565). On October 17, 1564, he declared that when one had received a benefice through a simoniacal transaction, even though he had been innocent of all wrong, he was *ipso facto* deprived of that benefice and it became reserved.[4]

4. *Quasi-simony*—In this case the reservation was directed at a crime which was often connected with simony. It seems that there were some clever members of the clergy who in taking examinations for benefices pretended to be some other cleric and thus enabled the latter unjustly to be credited with high marks. On November 27, 1557, Paul IV ruled that all who perpetrated such deceptions lost whatever benefices they possessed and in turn these were reserved to the Pope.[5]

5. *Failure to wear the clerical garb*—On January 9, 1589, Pope Sixtus V complained vehemently against the many clerics who were assuming the dress of the laity. He insisted that this condition be remedied. All the clerics who failed to heed this warning were to lose their benefices, which thereupon became reserved to the Holy See.[6] In 1725 Pope Benedict XIII issued a reservation along the same general principles.[7]

glottis Vaticanis, 1923-1939, vols. VII, VIII, and IX ed. cura et studio Emi. Iustiniani Card. Seredi), I, n. 94. This collection will hereafter be cited as *Fontes*.

[3] Const. *Cum ex apostolatus*, 27 ian. 1567, § 1—*Fontes*, I, n. 117.

[4] Const. *Romanum Pontificem*, § 2—*Fontes*, I, n. 106.

[5] Motu propr. *Inter caeteras*, §§ 1, 2— Fontes, I, n. 92.

[6] Const. *Cum sacrosanctam*, 3—*Fontes*, I, n. 167.

[7] Const. *Apostolicae Ecclesiae*, 2 Maii, 1725, § 2—*Fontes*, I, n. 286.

CHAPTER VI

EXEMPTIONS FROM THE RESERVATIONS

THE two preceding chapters have offered a detailed account of the development of the ecclesiastical legislation on reserved benefices. With the completion of this treatment one imagines a legal system whose most impressive feature is its vastness. Its huge framework seems to have encompassed almost every benefice. Barely visible in the distant background stands the well-nigh meaningless right of the local bishops, the founded intention of law that they can confer all the vacant benefices in their dioceses.

That picture, however, does not conform to reality. It lacks this conformity for the simple reason that it is not complete. It indicates all the major legislation on this subject but until some consideration is given to the benefices which were exempt from these laws, there can be no hope that the picture will be a true representation of the system of reserved benefices. Viewed in the light of these canonical exemptions a new perspective is revealed. The sharp lines of the reservations mellow and, though the system still remains quite vast, it becomes more and more evident that the background is important—that the local bishops still had a significant voice in the conferring of the vacant benefices in their dioceses.

ARTICLE 1. BENEFICES EXEMPT BY THE CANONICAL INTERPRETATION OF THE RESERVATIONS

No attempt will be made to exhaust this phase of the canonical interpretation. In the canonical commentary of this work a detailed discussion will be given to several interpretations which affect the present legislation of the Church. In this article the presentation will consist of but a few general indications of the limitations imposed on the reservations by this canonical interpretation.

The basis for every canonical interpretation on reserved benefices is the principle, " reservations are odious and hence subject to a strict interpretation." This axiom was first explicitly stated by Ionnaes Andreae.[1] By no means did it receive immediate universal acclaim, being a sharp controversial issue for several centuries. Gradually, however, the negative opinion was discarded and from the eighteenth century onwards the principle was universally accepted.[2]

The school of thought which denied this principle was led by Gonzalez and Lotterius.[3] They conceded that the reservation was something odious. But they immediately added that there are some laws which are both odious and favorable, and that it was in this category that they placed the reservation.[4] Then they maintained that the note that made it a favorable law (insofar as it was advantageous to worthy clerics) was the more powerful and determined the final classification. Their fault centered in the fact that they acknowledged the purpose of the legislator (to give the benefices to worthy clerics) as the determining factor of the law. That, of course, was incorrect. Actually, however, the entire discussion was confined to the field of pure theory. Neither Gonzalez nor Lotterius interpreted the reservations widely. To illustrate the truth of this statement, only these two shall be listed as authorities for the restrictive interpretations listed below.

Most authors list approximately a dozen of these restrictive interpretations. From this field three of the more important ones

[1] *Glossa ordinaria* ad v. "finitur"—c. 3, *de officio legati,* I, 15, in VI°: "...sed reservationes beneficiorum sunt odiosae propter duo; quia per eas datur via ad vacaturas et quia praeiudicant ordinariae potestati: igitur sunt restringendae."

[2] Reiffenstuel, *Ius canonicum universum,* lib. III, tit. V, n. 388; D'Annibale, *Summula theologiae moralis* (3rd ed., 3 vols., Romae, 1892), III, 34.

[3] Gonzalez, *De reservatione mensium,* proemium VI, nn. 1-74; Lotterius, *De re beneficiaria,* lib. II, q. XXVI.

[4] Gonzalez, *ibid.,* n. 45: "Est odiosa quia detrahitur potestati ordinariae ...negari non potest quin fit partim odiosa et partim favorabilis."

have been selected to indicate to the reader the general trend of this canonical interpretation. These three exceptions are:

1. *Manual benefices*—A manual benefice is one which is "*revocabile ad nutum superioris.*" Now even though a reservation stated that it affected all benefices, it did not reserve manual benefices.[5] Enjoying this same exemption were benefices which had been conferred not *in perpetuum* but for a specified time, e. g., for five years.[6] This immunity of manual benefices was quite important, for most of the benefices which belonged to the religious orders were manual.[7]

2. *Benefices subject to the right of lay patronage*—In like manner, even though a law explicitly reserved all benefices of a certain type, it did not include benefices subject to the right of lay patronage.[8]

3. Benefices which constituted the *mensa episcopalis*—The exemption also held for this type of benefice.[9]

ARTICLE 2. BENEFICES EXEMPT BY PARTICULAR LAW (CONCORDATS)

In the preceding pages attention has been focused on the *legal* system of reserved benefices as it existed from the thirteenth to the eighteenth centuries. That just about completes the legal and canonical content of this historical section. All the universal laws as well as an adequate sampling of the particular reservations have been outlined. The fundamental principles of interpretation have been illustrated. Yet, a true evaluation of the system of reserved benefices has not been completely achieved. The laws which have been studied represent the ideal. Obviously, of course, it is one thing for the Pope to reserve a benefice, but an entirely different thing for his subjects to obey that com-

[5] Lotterius, *op. cit.*, lib. I, q. VII, n. 22; Gonzalez, gloss. V, pars VI, n. 9.

[6] Gonzalez, *op. cit.*, proemium VI, nn. 10, 19, 57.

[7] Lotterius, *op. cit.*, lib. I, q. XXXIII, nn. 4, 8.

[8] Gonzalez, *op. cit.*, gloss XVIII, n. 2.

[9] Gonzalez, *op. cit.*, gloss V, pars VI, nn. 63, 64.

mand. It is with this in mind that the writer now turns to the practical question of the effect of all these reservations.

The better method of treating this phase of the actual observance of the papal reservations would be the direct method, i. e., to directly consider the history of the resistance in the various countries.[10] Such an involved method, however, is beyond the scope of this work. Instead, an indirect method will be employed—the consideration of the Concordats. Since the Concordats were a direct result of this resistance to the reservations, the reader can deduce to some extent the resistance itself. From the many Concordats which mitigated the reservations three of the earlier and more important ones have been selected.

1. *The German Concordat*—During the first half of the fifteenth century several temporary (of five years duration) agreements were reached between the Holy See and the German Emperors.[11] It was not until the reign of Nicholas V (1447-1455), however, that a permanent understanding was accomplished. This pact, commonly called the Concordat of Vienna, was confirmed on March 26, 1448.[12] The primary concession granted by Nicholas concerned the conferring of bishoprics and archbishoprics. When one of these sees became vacant, the German clergy were to hold a canonical election and submit the name of their candidate to the Pope, who was to confirm him unless he considered him unsuitable for the position. With reference to the minor ecclesiastical benefices, many were reserved to the Pope. The most extensive reservation affected all benefices which became vacant during the months of January, March, May, July, September, and November. Also reserved were the following: benefices vacant at the Holy See, benefices of the cardinals

[10] The writer has made some survey concerning the historical conditions in several of the more important countries in Europe and would estimate that prior to the mitigation of the general law by means of Concordats no more than fifty percent of the reserved benefices were conferred by the Holy See.

[11] *Mansi*, XXVII, 1189-1191.

[12] *Bullarium Romanum*, V, 96 sq.

and officials of the Holy See, benefices of one promoted to the episcopacy, the major dignity in the cathedral church, and the principal dignity in the collegiate church.

2. *The French Concordat*—There were several agreements between the Popes and the French Kings during the fifteenth century which theoretically settled the question of reserved benefices.[13] Actually, however, they did little to pacify the French antagonism towards the reservations. It was only on August 16, 1516, when Leo X confirmed the French Concordat,[14] that this trouble was settled. The Church fared rather poorly in this compromise. Only one real reservation survived, namely, the *Licet ecclesiarum.* The only other power retained by the Pope concerned the conferring of bishoprics. In this matter no one was to receive such a provision unless he had been confirmed by the Pontiff.

3. *The English Concordat*—The question of reserved benefices in England was solved in the year 1418 when an agreement was reached between Pope Martin V (1417-1431) and King Henry V (1413-1422).[15] Considering the opposition towards papal provisions evidenced by the previous English Kings,[16] the provisions of this pact were surprisingly favorable to the Church. It reserved the following minor benefices: those which became vacant during the months of January, March, May, July, September, and November; benefices vacant *apud Sedem Apostolicam;* benefices of the cardinals and of the officials of the Holy See. Martin V, however, made an important concession regarding the appointment of bishops. In this matter the English King was granted the right of nominating his selection. The Pope was to confirm the candidate if he seemed suitable.

[13] E. g., Council of Constance, Sess. 43, sectio 15—*Mansi,* XXVII, 1184.

[14] Fifth Lateran Council, sess. 11—*Mansi,* XXXII, 947.

[15] *Mansi,* XXVII, 1193.

[16] E. g., 25 Edward III, stat. 3—Evans, *A collection of statutes* (7 vols., London, 1817), V, 11; 3 Richard II, c. 3—Evans, V, 13.

CHAPTER VII

Reservations In the Last Three Centuries

It may here be recalled that the legal and historical development of most of the reservations, i. e., those contained in the *Regulae Cancellariae,* was traced only till the time of Clement XI (1700-1721). But from that period until the promulgation of the Code not one change is to be found in the common law of the Church in this regard. The *Regulae Cancellariae* were reissued *verbatim* by the Popes. Furthermore, none of the constitutions containing the penal reservations were withdrawn.

Really there was no need for a change in the common law of the Church. Most of the countries had their concordats which could be and were adapted to meet any pressing needs.[1] But more important as a reason for this immutability of the universal law of the Church was the fact that the reservations themselves had lost much of their original force. Not that this entailed any fundamental change in the nature of the reservation. Rather the change concerned the manner of conferring the reserved benefice.

The Roman Curia had been in complete charge of the provision of reserved benefices until the time of the Council of Trent. Trent, however, emphasized the necessity of conducting an examination to determine the most worthy candidate for every vacant parish church.[2] In 1566 Pius V explained in his Constitution, *In conferendis,*[3] that the bishop was to conduct this examination even for the parochial churches which were reserved communicating to the Pope the name of the cleric whom he

[1] For a thorough treatment of these concordats consult Lindon, *op. cit.,* pp. 170-230.

[2] Sess. XXIV, *de ref.,* c. 18.

[3] *Bullarium Romanum,* VII, 551, n. 1.

deemed most worthy.[4] Thus the most important element in the conferring of reserved parochial benefices, the selection of the candidate, was once more placed in the power of the local bishops.

With the promulgation of the Code of Canon Law in the Constitution *Providentissima Mater Ecclesia* of Pope Benedict XV on May 27, 1917, and its subsequent binding force over the universal Church on May 19, 1918, the system of reserved benefices was completely revised. The present law of the Church states that only those benefices are reserved which are mentioned in canon 1435.

[4] *Loc. cit.*: "...electos nobis vel successoribus nostris...pro collatione obtinenda intra quattuor mensium spatium a die vacationis."

PART II

CANONICAL COMMENTARY

CHAPTER VIII

Preliminary Canonical Considerations

Article 1. Nature of the Benefice in Canon Law

Can. 1409. **Beneficium ecclesiasticum est ens iuridicum a competente ecclesiastica auctoritate in perpetuum constitutum seu erectum, constans officio sacro et iure percipiendi reditus ex dote officio adnexos.**

Since the benefice is an institution of ecclesiastical origin,[1] the Church has the right not only of determining what constitutes a benefice but also of changing these requirements as she sees fit. Before the issuance of the Code she refrained more or less from any official definition of the benefice. Nevertheless the Church gave a sufficient number of practical decisions, e. g., Rota decisions and replies of the Sacred Congregation of the Council, to guide the canonists in their formation of the basic concept of this institution. It is surprising to note how constant this concept of the benefice remained throughout the centuries preceding the Code. The one major exception to this stability concerned the question of the subjective perpetuity of the benefice, i. e., the tenure of office of the incumbent. With the promulgation of the Code, however, that question was definitely settled and the way cleared for an even more definite concept of the ecclesiastical benefice.

Canon 1409 describes the ecclesiastical benefice as a juridical entity permanently established or erected by the competent

[1] Nicolaus Garcia, *Tractatus de beneficiis*, pars V, cap. I, n. 3; Melchior Lotterius, *De re beneficiaria*, lib. I, q. IV, n. 54; Petrus Leurenius, *Forum beneficiale* (Venetiis, 1742), p. 3, q. 12; Petrus Scavini, *Theologia moralis universa ad mentem S. Alphonsi M. de Ligorio* (4 vols., 11th ed., Mediolani, 1869), III, 564, n. 677; Wernz, *Ius decretalium*, vol. II, *Ius constitutionis Ecclesiae* (Romae, 1899), p. 351, n. 245.

ecclesiastical authority consisting of a sacred office and the right of receiving from the dowry the revenue attached to the office. A thorough consideration will be given to this description, because it embodies those ecclesiastical offices which form the subject of this thesis. Contrariwise, if a given ecclesiastical office lacks even one of the details mentioned in the above canon, it is not a benefice and hence is not affected by the reservations in the Code. In all, canon 1409 postulates five distinct elements which are characteristic of the ecclesiastical benefice.

a) The benefice is a *juridic entity*. This is another way of stating that the benefice is a moral person.[2] Moral personality stands, of course, in contradistinction to physical personality. It denotes something which by a fiction of law is considered the subject of rights and obligations. As canon 99 mentions, the benefice is a non-collegiate moral person. A collegiate moral person is one which is composed of at least three physical persons.[3] The benefice is composed not of physical persons but rather of the sacred office and the right to the revenue attached to the office.

b) The benefice must be constituted or *erected by the competent ecclesiastical authority*. Coronata has reached the one feasible solution, namely, that the two terms employed by the Code, i. e., to constitute and to erect, do not signify different acts but point to the same basic act.[4] They denote any positive act whereby the ecclesiastical authority establishes a moral person. This establishment should ordinarily be accomplished by a legal document describing the place, the sacred office, the dowry, and the rights and duties of the beneficiary.[5] Though Pistocchi seems to regard this document as a requirement for the valid

[2] Marius Pistocchi, *De re beneficiali* (Taurini: Marietti, 1928), p. 7. Cf. canon 99.

[3] Canon 100, § 2.

[4] Coronata, *Institutiones iuris canonici*, II, 357, n. 972.

[5] Canon 1418.

erection of the benefice,[6] most authors have adopted the opposite view.[7] This common stand of the authors seems correct because canon 1418 neither expressly nor equivalently states that this document is necessary for validity and therefore in view of canon 11 [8] it is not required for validity. This same opinion has received support from a private reply of the Pontifical Commission for the Authentic Interpretation of the Code regarding certain parochial benefices in the United States.[9]

The primary purpose in stating that the ecclesiastical power is the only authority competent to establish a benefice is to notify the State that it has no right in this matter. This doctrine, which is as ancient as the benefice itself, has been repeated again and again by the Church. One of the constituent elements of the benefice is the sacred office, which of its nature is spiritual. Now since the Church has been entrusted with the exclusive care of the spiritual realm, she alone can establish the ecclesiastical benefice. Thus the State could construct a chapel and endow it with lucrative resources. But there its competence would terminate, and unless the Church intervened, that institution could never attain the status of a benefice.[10]

At times the wording of certain past concordats might seem to indicate some relaxation on the part of the Church in this regard.

[6] Pistocchi, *De re beneficiali*, p. 130.

[7] Coronata, *Institutiones iuris canonici*, II, 369; Felix Cappello, *Summa iuris canonici* (3 vols., Vol. II, Romae: Universitas Gregoriana, 1930), II, 477, n. 869; Vermeersch-Creusen, *Epitome iuris canonici* (3 vols., Mechliniae: H. Dessain, vol. I, 5th ed., 1934; vol. II, 5th ed., 1936; vol. III, 6th ed., 1937), II, 528; Linden, *op. cit.*, p. 240: Nicholas Connolly, *The canonical erection of parishes*, Catholic University of America, Canon Law Studies, n. 114 (Washington, D. C.: Catholic University, 1938), p. 71.

[8] "Irritantes aut inhabilitantes eae tantum leges habendae sunt, quibus aut actum esse nullum aut inhabilem esse personam expresse vel aequivalenter statuitur."

[9] Reply of Sept. 26, 1921—Bouscaren, *The canon law digest* (2 vols. and supplement, 1934-1941, Milwaukee: Bruce), I, 149.

[10] Ayrinhac, *Administrative legislation in the new Code of Canon Law* (New York: Longmans, Green, 1930), p. 312.

That, however, is not the case. When the Church agrees with a particular State that she will not establish any new parishes (the parish is a benefice) without the consent of that State, she is not conceding the State the right to share her power of establishing ecclesiastical benefices. In such concordats the Church merely safeguards the recognition of whatever civil effects the State provides for the moral persons in its territory.[11]

Canon 1409 rules that the benefice must be established by the *competent* ecclesiastical authority, and not simply by any ecclesiastical authority whatever. As supreme ruler of the Church, the Roman Pontiff enjoys the immediate right of establishing any and all types of benefices. With the exception of the more important benefices, e. g., episcopal sees, the Pope seldom uses this power. Most of the minor benefices are established by the local ordinaries, who enjoy ordinary power in this matter.[12]

c) The ecclesiastical benefice must be *permanently* established. Mention has been made of the fact that a benefice is a moral person, and it is from this source that the note of perpetuity flows.[13] When, however, one repeats the common expression that a benefice is perpetual, it must be interpreted as subject to two limitations. First, this note of perpetuity does not necessarily imply a ceaseless continuity of operative effect. Thus the office of vicar capitular does not possess such a continuity, for its operative effect depends on conditions which of their nature recur only at indefinite intervals. Yet it is a perpetual office insofar as it has been permanently established by the proper ecclesiastical authority.[14] The second limitation to this note of permanency is based on the distinction between subjective and objective per-

[11] Coronata, *Institutiones iuris canonici,* II, 356, ftn. 2.

[12] Pistocchi, *De re beneficiali,* p. 43.

[13] Canon 102: "Persona moralis, natura sua, perpetua est..."

[14] Ojetti, *Commentarium in codicem iuris canonici* (4 vols., Romae: Universitas Gregoriana, 1927-1931), IV, 3, ftn. 1; Claeys-Bouuaert et Simenon, *Manuale iuris canonici* (2d ed., Gandae et Leodii; Seminarium Gandavense et Leodiense, 1926), p. 565.

petuity. Objective perpetuity signifies that the office once established cannot cease to exist of its own accord but only through the intervention of the proper authority. Subjective perpetuity signifies that the individual appointed to the office must receive a permanent tenure of office. This subjective perpetuity prohibits two types of appointments; the office cannot be conferred on the incumbent for a limited period of time, e. g., for three years, nor can it be conferred with the provision that it can be revoked at the discretion of the one conferring.[15] The majority of the pre-Code canonists insisted that an office could not be a benefice unless it enjoyed both types of perpetuity.[16] The Code, however, has canonized the opinion that the only perpetuity demanded by the benefice is objective perpetuity.

d) Every benefice must contain a *sacred office.* The importance of the sacred office, which is the foundation of the benefice (*beneficium datur propter officium*),[17] has always been stressed by the theologians. In explaining the nature of a sacred office present day canonists universally identify it with the term *ecclesiastical office* as described in the fourth title of the second book of the Code.[18] The present law of the Church declares that the ecclesiastical office may be understood in a wide sense or in a strict sense. The former embraces any function which is lawfully exercised for a spiritual end, e. g., the collecting of alms for an ecclesiastical institution. In the strict sense an ecclesiastical office is any function firmly established, either by divine or ecclesiastical authority, to be conferred according to the norms of the sacred canons and bearing with it some participation of ecclesiast-

[15] Ballerini-Palmieri, *Opus theologicum morale* (7 vols., Prati, 1889-1893), IV, 187.

[16] Leurenius, *Forum beneficiale*, p. 1, q. 4; Riganti, In regul. IX, sectio II, n. 77; Sanguinetti, *Institutiones iuris ecclesiastici privati* (Romae, 1884), p. 355; Casimir Gennari, *Quistioni canoniche* (2nd ed., Romae, 1908), p. 692.

[17] Reiffenstuel, *Ius canonicum universum*, lib. III, tit. V, sectio I, n. 10.

[18] Pistocchi, *op. cit.*, p. 11; Cappello, *Summa iuris canonici*, II, 470; A. De Meester, *Juris canonici et juris canonico-civilis compendium* (nova ed., 3 vols. in 4, Brugis: Desclée, 1921-1928), III, 322.

ical power, whether of orders or of jurisdiction.[19] The Code establishes the presumption that the ecclesiastical office is to be interpreted in the strict sense unless the opposite is apparent in the context.[20] Since there is nothing in the context of canon 1409 to destroy this presumption, the benefice must include a sacred office in the strict meaning of the term. Thus any office which can be conferred on the laity, e. g., the office of sacristan, organist, or sexton, can not provide the foundation for a benefice under the present law.[21] Furthermore many offices which are conferred on the clergy are *per se* equally insufficient, e. g., professorships in theological seminaries, because *per se* they involve no power of jurisdiction or of orders.

e) The benefice must include the right of the incumbent to receive from an endowment or from some other equivalent source the revenues and returns which are attached to the office. The canonists have always stressed as the important element of the benefice the right to the revenue. Wernz-Vidal view it as the element whereby the benefice is formally constituted.[22] This right to the revenue naturally presupposes some source from which the revenue flows, namely the endowment. Canon 1409 in describing the benefice merely mentions its existence. A complete description, however, is contained in canons 1410 and 1415. As Connolly notes, pre-Code canonists had a rigid concept of the endowment, emphasizing the necessity both of its certainty and of its sufficiency.[23] The Code has departed from such a rigid view of the endowment and by thus enlarging its concept has amplified the extension of the ecclesiastical benefice. Conse-

[19] Canon 145, § 1.

[20] Canon 145, § 2.

[21] Canon 118: "Soli clerici possunt potestatem sive ordinis sive iurisdictionis ecclesiasticae et beneficia et pensiones ecclesiasticas obtinere."

[22] Wernz-Vidal, *Ius canonicum*, II, 166.

[23] Connolly, *The canonical erection of parishes*, p. 44; Leurenius, *Forum beneficiale*, p. 2, q. 7.

quently many offices which before the Code were not considered benefices must now be viewed as such.[24]

Canon 1410 rules that the endowment of the benefice may be formed by goods owned by the moral person, by definite payments owed by some family or moral person, by reliable voluntary contributions of the faithful which accrue to the rector, by stole fees within the limits imposed by diocesan statutes or lawful custom, or by distributions connected with active choir service, to the exclusion however, of one third of these if the entire beneficial revenue consists of such distributions alone. Where it is a question of establishing a parochial benefice, the dowry assumes an even wider scope. Here the proper ecclesiastical authority can erect a parochial benefice even if the fitting dowry mentioned above is lacking, provided that he prudently foresees that the necessary income will not be lacking.[25]

ARTICLE 2. THE RIGHT OF THE POPE TO RESERVE BENEFICES

Can. 1431. **Ius Romano Pontifici est beneficia in universa Ecclesia conferendi eorumque collationem sibimet reservandi.**

This canon repeats a statement of doctrine which has been accepted by all Catholic theologians and canonists.[26] From the theological viewpoint this doctrine is so certain that to deny it would be altogether rash and erroneous.[27] It will be noticed that the Code recognizes this papal power as extending over the universal Church, which includes the Oriental Church. Nor is this at variance with the statement of canon 1, because it is a question of a doctrine of the Church, namely the power given to Peter when he was constituted the first supreme ruler of the entire Church. Furthermore, this papal power extends to every bene-

24 Wernz-Vidal, *Ius canonicum,* II, 162, ftn. 1.

25 Canon 1415, § 3.

26 Wernz-Vidal, *Ius canonicum,* II, n. 225.

27 Bouix, *De parocho,* p. 312: "... atque illud negare temerarium prorsus esset atque erroneum ..."

fice in the Church. It suffers none of the limitations imposed by positive law on the actual reservations in the Code, e. g., manual benefices.[28]

The mere announcement of this doctrine may fail to impress the reader with its potentially far-reaching consequences. Yet this very doctrine really means that the Pope, if he deemed it advisable, could reserve every benefice in the Church. Naturally such a course of action could be justified only by the most extraordinary circumstances. So far no Pope has ever employed this potent prerogative. Furthermore, it seems altogether improbable that any of the future successors of St. Peter will ever use such a power. Notwithstanding this practical consideration, its very possibility may prompt one to wonder why anyone, even the Roman Pontiff, should possess such power over all the ecclesiastical benefices.

The answer to such a query is, of course, quite simple. The Pope possesses such power because Christ willed that he should possess it. Christ's intention in this regard is clearly evidenced by the cumulative force of four of His acts. First, Christ established His Church as a perfect society.[29] Secondly, He selected the monarchical form of government for His Church. Thirdly, He established the Apostle Peter as the first supreme ruler of this Church. Finally, He decreed that the power given to Peter should be perpetuated in the Church.

Though it is beyond the scope of this work to present the complete treatment and proof of these four facts,[30] it will prove useful

28 Canon 1435, § 2 exempts manual benefices from the present reservations.

29 Ottaviani defines a perfect society: "Societas iuridice perfecta ea est quae bonum in suo ordine completum tamquam finem habens, ac media omnia ad illud consequendum iure possidens, est in suo ordine sibi sufficiens et independens, id est plene autonoma."—*Institutiones iuris publici ecclesiastici* (2nd ed., 2 vols., Typis Polyglottis Vaticanis, 1935-1936), I, n. 25.

30 The reader may consult any of the standard authors either on the *Ius Publicum Ecclesiasticum* or on Fundamental Dogmatic Theology for a detailed study of the nature of the Church.

to indicate the general trend of the arguments adduced to prove them. What is of importance to this work, however, is to show the particular application of these four points to the problem at hand, namely, the papal right to reserve benefices.

Since the end determines the classification of a society,[31] the Church must be regarded as a perfect society, because it has been endowed with the highest ultimate end in the spiritual realm, the eternal salvation of souls.[32] Furthermore, Christ has supplied the spiritual means for the attainment of that end, particularly the sacraments and the Sacrifice of the Mass.

Now, precisely because the Church is a perfect society it possesses certain inherent rights. Jurists base the existence of these rights on the fact that its perfect end would be meaningless unless the society had the right to demand those things which are necessary or useful for the attainment of that end, provided that the things demanded do not pertain to an end of an equal or higher order.[33] It should be noted here that if any given act provides a means whereby the Church may lawfully attain her end, she is justified in exacting such an act. Nor has any human society the right to deny this claim, because no human society, even though it is a perfect society, has an end equal or superior to the end of the Church.[34]

What, then, is to be said of the right of appointing men to ecclesiastical benefices? Can this be considered as a necessary or useful means towards the salvation of souls? If such is the case, the Church alone possesses the right to make these appointments.

It will be recalled that the foundation of the ecclesiastical benefice is the sacred office. This sacred office implies either the

[31] Cavagnis, *Institutiones iuris publici ecclesiastici* (4th ed., 3 vols., Romae, 1906), I, p. 35, n. 58; Ottaviani, *op. cit.*, I, n. 25.

[32] Mark XVI: 15, 16; Luke XXIV: 47.

[33] Ottaviani, *Institutiones iuris publici ecclesiastici*, I, 78.

[34] Ottaviani, *op. cit.*, I, 146.

power of orders, the power of jurisdiction, or both. Now, both of these powers are necessary for the proper attainment of the Church's end. The power of orders is primarily concerned with the bestowal of graces, which constitute the proximate means of salvation.[35] The power of jurisdiction enables the Church to guide her members to their final end by enacting laws, making judgments, administering the temporal goods of the Church, ruling the members, and punishing those who are delinquent. Thus the benefice is founded on the sacred office, which is without question a means employed by the Church for the salvation of souls. Therefore one is compelled to conclude that the ecclesiastical benefice is under the exclusive jurisdiction of the Church and that she alone can appoint the one who is to rule the benefice. If some power other than the Church, for example the State, had the right to appoint the beneficiary, of what value would the benefice be to the Church? The State could, and indeed often would, appoint men either unwilling or unsuitable to dispense the Church's most valuable means for the attainment of her end. To deny to the Church the right to appoint the incumbents of her benefices is tantamount to denying her perfection.

With the Church possessing the right of appointing men to her benefices, the question now arises: Who in the Church is empowered to confer these benefices? Once more the answer has been determined by a voluntary act of the Church's divine Founder. Christ could have established His Church under one of several forms of government. As a matter of fact, however, He selected the monarchical form and established Peter as the first supreme ruler of the Church.[36] Upon him Christ bestowed the jurisdiction to rule the entire Church. That, of course, gave

[35] Cappello, *Summa iuris publici ecclesiastici* (2nd ed., Romae: Apud Aedes Universitatis Gregorianae, 1928), p. 418.

[36] Matt. XVI: 18, 19: "And I say to thee, thou art Peter, and upon this rock I will build my Church, and the gates of hell shall not prevail against it. And I will give thee the keys of the kingdom of heaven; and whatsoever thou shalt bind on earth shall be bound in heaven, and whatsoever thou shalt loose on earth shall be loosed in heaven."

Peter the right of conferring and reserving all the ecclesiastical offices in the Church.

Furthermore, Christ ruled that the supreme power which He gave to Peter was not to cease with the death of Peter, but was to be perpetuated in his successors.[37] Christ's intention in this matter is clear from the fact that He constituted Peter the foundation of the Church. Naturally the foundation must last as long as the building which it is to support. Now, since the Church is perpetual,[38] it follows that Christ intended that Peter should have successors with equally supreme jurisdiction over the entire Church. From tradition it is clear that these successors of Peter have been the Roman Pontiffs.[39] Because of this succession the present reigning Pontiff enjoys the supreme jurisdiction given to Peter. Due to this power of ruling the Church he can freely reserve any and all benefices in the universal Church.

It is interesting to note that a formal and complete declaration of the papal power over the ecclesiastical benefice was not issued by the papacy until the year 1265. In that year Pope Clement IV issued the decretal *Licet ecclesiarum,* which contained an accurate description of the papal right to the plenary disposition of all ecclesiastical benefices.[40] Many of the opponents of the Church, particularly Justinus Febronius,[41] have interpreted the rather late appearance of such a declaration of papal power as a proof that the Popes of the twelfth and thirteenth centuries fraudulently usurped this power. That view, however, is erron-

[37] Concilium Vaticanum, Const. *Pastor aeternus,* cap. 1.

[38] Matt. XXVIII: 19.

[39] Cappello, *Summa iuris publici ecclesiastici,* p. 430.

[40] C. 2, *De praebendis et dignitatibus,* III, 4, in VI°: "Licet ecclesiarum, personatuum, dignitatum, aliorumque beneficiorum ecclesiasticorum plenaria dispositio ad Romanum noscatur Pontificem pertinere, ita quod non solum cum vacant potest de iure conferre, verum etiam ius in ipsis tribuere vacaturis..."

[41] *De statu ecclesiae et legitima potestate Romani Pontificis* (2 vols., Frankfurt, 1763), I, 460 sq.

eous and cannot be tolerated in light of the fundamental theological argument which proves this power.

ARTICLE 3. CANONICAL EFFECTS OF THE RESERVATION

Most of the canonists of the last few centuries have defined the reservation as the act whereby the Pope appropriates to himself a benefice which is about to become vacant.[42] The Code has effected no change whatever in this basic concept of the reservation.[43] Yet, no matter how closely that definition is analyzed, it fails to provide complete information about the reserved benefice. For example, it gives no indication concerning the validity or invalidity of provisions made by ecclesiastical superiors in violation of the reservation. Again, there is no mention of the duration of the withdrawal of the benefice. It will be the purpose of this chapter to view these and other canonical aspects of the reserved benefice. In general, the canonical effects of the reservation may be grouped as follows:

a. *The Apostolic See alone is competent to confer validly a reserved benefice*

Prior to the Code the canonists distinguished two types of reservations: the reservation without any invalidating clause (called the *simple* reservation) and the reservation with an invalidating clause. All agreed that this latter type invalidated all contrary provisions of benefices, even such provisions as were made by one totally unaware of the existence of the reservation. The efficacy of the simple reservation, however, was the subject of much discussion. The more prevalent opinion held that the simple reservation did not render invalid the provisions of benefices made in violation of its prescriptions, but merely rendered

[42] A comprehensive list of these authors will be found in Lux, p. 4.

[43] Wernz-Vidal, *Ius canonicum*, II, 251, n. 231; Pistocchi, *De re beneficiali*, p. 182; Cocchi, *Commentarium in Codicem iuris canonici*, III, *De rebus* (Romae: Marietti, 1925), 243; Coronata, *Institutiones iuris canonici*, II, 385.

such acts illicit.[44] Completely opposed to this stand was the opinion advanced by Leurenius (d. 1273) and Lotterius, (d. after 1632), namely, that the simple reservation invalidated all such provisions.[45] Between these two extremes was the view of Garcia (d. after 1613) and Reiffenstuel (d. 1703), who maintained that the simple reservation invalidated such provisions placed against it by one who knew of the reservation but not those placed by one who was unaware of the reservation.[46] Not much emphasis should be placed on this dispute, for it was more or less confined to the field of legal theory. The so-called simple reservation was almost a non-entity. It existed primarily in the minds of the canonists. And the few simple reservations which did emanate from the Roman Pontiffs appeared in the earlier centuries of this institution. Riganti (1661-1735) noted the appearance of a simple reservation as late as the year 1655,[47] but this must be regarded as exceptional. There seems to be no evidence of the simple reservation after that year. This lack of practical importance on the part of the simple reservation is also reflected in the writings of many of the Italian authors. It should be remembered that these authors were quite naturally interested in the papal reservations, for Italy was the only nation in which most of the general reservations were not modified by concordats.[48] Yet, despite their evident concern, many of the Italian authors who give a fairly complete treatment to the subject of reserved benefices, e. g., Scavini, Simeone, Ballerini, Santi, and Sanguinetti, never even mention the existence of the simple reservation. They

44 Riganti, In regul. I, sectio I, nn. 77-80; Schmalzgrueber, *Ius ecclesiasticum universum,* III, pars I, n. 216; Wernz, *Ius decretalium,* II, n. 333, IV a; D'Annibale, *Summula theologiae moralis,* III, 35, ftn. 6.

45 Leurenius, *Forum beneficiale,* II, q. 522, n. 2; Lotterius, *De re beneficiali,* II, q. 26, nn. 2-4.

46 Garcia, *Tractatus de beneficiis,* pars V, cap. I, n. 409; Reiffenstuel, *Ius canonicum universum,* lib. III, tit. V, n. 384.

47 Riganti, In regul. II, sectio III, n. 82.

48 Sebastianelli, *Praelectiones iuris canonici* (2nd ed., 3 vols., Romae, 1905), I, 209; Wernz, *Ius decretalium,* II, 455.

would hardly have ignored this institution if it had had any practical importance.

Of the three opinions concerning the efficacy of the simple reservation, the first opinion, which held that provisions made in violation of the simple reservation were illicit but valid, was the most probable. Certainly it was the opinion to follow in practice, since the reservation is subject to a strict interpretation.

Those who were responsible for the Code of Canon Law definitely precluded any similar dispute under the present law of the Church. On the one hand, canon 11 supplies the general principle which is to determine the invalidating effects of any given law in the Code.[49] On the other hand, canon 1434 specifically states that all those who are inferior to the Apostolic See confer reserved benefices invalidly.[50] Thus the violation of any of the present reservations always affects the validity of the provision. There is no longer any grounds for distinctions. Nor does it make any difference who confers the reserved benefice, whether he be a cardinal, a bishop, or any other dignitary of the Church.

It should be noted that whereas canon 1431 speaks of the power of the *Roman Pontiff* to reserve benefices, canon 1435 mentions the power of the *Apostolic See* to confer them. Thus it is not only the Roman Pontiff personally who can confer the reserved benefices [51] but also those congregations and offices through which the Pope is accustomed to expedite the conferring of this type of benefice.[52] This notion is merely brought to the

[49] Canon II: "Irritantes aut inhabilitantes eae tantum leges habendae sunt, quibus aut actum esse nullum aut inhabilem esse personam expresse vel aequivalenter statuitur."

[50] Canon 1434: "Beneficia Sedi Apostolicae reservata ab inferioribus invalide conferuntur."

[51] Canon 7.

[52] The following are accustomed to participate in the conferring of reserved benefices: Consistorial Congregation (c. 248), Congregation for the Propagation of the Faith (c. 293, par. 2), Congregation for extraordinary ecclesiastical affairs (c. 255), and the Apostolic Chancery (c. 260).

reader's attention here; it will be discussed in a later chapter devoted to the consideration of the actual conferring of reserved benefices.

b. *The prohibition against the exchange or the union of reserved benefices*

Closely associated with the direct conferring of reserved benefices is the exchange of benefices of which one or both are reserved to the Holy See. The present legislation regulating the exchange of ecclesiastical benefices is contained in canons 1487 and 1488. The former canon explicitly rules that the Ordinary cannot admit an exchange where one or both of the benefices involved are reserved to the Apostolic See.[53] This note of invalidity in the present case is evident not from the canon in question,[54] but rather from canon 1434. The reason for this statement is that the exchange of its very nature includes not only the acceptance of the two benefices involved but also the *conferring* of these same benefices.[55] In other words, whenever any ecclesiastical superior admits the exchange of two benefices, he is actually conferring both of these benefices. Now, since canon 1434 rules that the Apostolic See is the only authority which can confer reserved benefices validly, it follows that the Apostolic See is the only authority which can validly admit the exchange involving a reserved benefice. Thus, if the local Ordinary admits an ex-

[53] Canon 1487, § 3: " Beneficiorum permutatio nequit admitti ab Ordinario si utrumque aut alterutrum beneficium sit Sedi Apostolicae reservatum."

[54] Canon 11 states that only those laws are to be considered invalidating or disqualifying in which it is explicitly or equivalently stated that an act is null or that a person is incapable (*inhabilis*) of acting. Now, paragraph 3 of canon 1487 contains no such explicit or equivalent expression. All that it states is that the exchange "admitti nequit." As Vermeersch-Creusen (*Epitome iuris canonici*, I, p. 101, n. 103) correctly remark, " Cum in lege quis dicitur quidpiam facere *non posse*, nondum exprimitur inhabilitas; verba ista sunt, per se, mere prohibentia."

[55] D'Annibale, *Summula theologiae moralis*, III, 63, n. 60; Saint-Leitner, *Praelectiones iuris canonici* (5 vols. in 3, Ratisbonae, 1898-1899), III, tit. XIX, p. 191; Coronata, *Institutiones iuris canonici*, II, 424, n. 1021.

[56] Canon 1414, § 1: " Beneficia consistorialia una Sedes Apostolica erigit."

change in which one or both of the benefices are reserved, that exchange is invalid.

Turning now to the consideration of the union of reserved benefices, it is at once apparent that the local Ordinary has no power to unite those reserved benefices which he cannot erect, namely, consistorial benefices[56] and dignities in cathedral and collegiate chapters.[57] These are completely beyond the authority of the local superiors and the Holy See is the only authority capable of uniting them.[58] Furthermore, a similar limitation restricts the local Ordinary from uniting any other reserved benefices, e. g., parochial benefices reserved to the Holy See, for canon 1424 rules that the Ordinary cannot unite reserved benefices with any other benefice whatever.[59] This prohibits every type of union, whether it be *unio exstinctiva, unio aeque principalis,* or *unio minus principalis*. As Pistocchi remarks,[60] this canon extinguishes the faculty given to local bishops by the Council of Trent whereby they could unite reserved benefices in certain stated circumstances.[61]

This legislation of the Code prohibiting the uniting of reserved benefices by the local Ordinaries is logically necessitated by the nature and the purpose of the reservation. The reservation, it will be recalled, withdraws the benefice from the power of the local Ordinary and thus appropriates for the Apostolic See the exclusive right of conferring that benefice. Now, if the local Ordinary were free to unite this reserved benefice with another, he could, at least in an indirect manner, weaken the acquired right by uniting with the reserved benefice a benefice with an insufficient endowment. It is to avoid such infringements upon

[57] Canon 394, § 2: "Erectio dignitatum Sedi Apostolicae reservatur."

[58] Sipos, *Enchiridion iuris canonici* (Pecs [Hungary], 1926), p. 730; Coronata, *Institutiones iuris canonici*, II, p. 369, n. 979.

[59] Canon 1424: "Ordinarii nunquam possunt beneficia quaevis unire ... vel Sedi Apostolicae reservata cum aliis quibuslibet."

[60] *De re beneficiali*, p. 99.

[61] Concilium Tridentinum, Sessio XXI, *de ref.*, cap. 5.

the acquired right of the Holy See that the Code forbids the local Ordinaries to unite any reserved benefices.[62]

What would be the legal consequences if the local Ordinary should unite a reserved benefice in violation of canon 1424? Both Blat and Pistocchi insist that such a union would be null and void.[63] Their contention seems quite correct. It is true that even the strong terminology of canon 1424, " Ordinarii nunquam possunt," does not necessarily decree the invalidity of acts against this canon. But if canon 1434 is carefully analyzed, there is every reason to believe that it equivalently decrees the nullity of such a union of reserved benefices. This latter canon speaks directly of the invalidity of the *conferring* of reserved benefices. Yet, as Pistocchi notes,[64] it requires more power to unite a benefice than it does to confer it. Thus, if canon 1434 states that the ordinary collators cannot validly confer a reserved benefice, it seems probable that the same canon is implicitly expressing the invalidity of the union of a reserved benefice attempted by anyone inferior to the Holy See. This same conclusion is evidenced in the definition of a reservation. The accepted definition merely states that it is " avocatio beneficii vacaturi per Romanum Pontificem ad se facta." Now, the withdrawal not only implies that the local Ordinary cannot confer it, but also that he cannot dispose of it in any manner, e. g., by exchange or by union. Such considerations seem to corroborate the doctrine of Blat and Pistocchi.

The Code has not explicitly prohibited such other means whereby local Ordinaries might make some disposition regarding reserved benefices, e. g., by means of a division, through a dismemberment, by way of a conversion, or in virtue of a transfer

62 Blat, *Commentarium textus Codicis iuris canonici*, III^2, 401; Augustine, *A commentary on the new Code of canon law* (8 vols., St. Louis: Herder, Vol. VI, 1921), VI, 504.

63 Blat, *op. cit.*, III^2, 400; Pistocchi, *De re beneficiali*, p. 94: "Dantur, hoc canone, conditiones plurimae, quae si non observentur, legitimae non evadunt, et validae uniones beneficiorum ab Ordinariis decretae."

64 *De re beneficiali*, p. 99.

of the beneficial see from one locality to another.[65] Nevertheless one must hold that the local Ordinaries cannot use such means of disposing a reserved benefice. This restriction is deduced from the similar restriction placed on the conferring, exchange, and union of reserved benefices.[66]

c. *The duration of the withdrawal of the benefice from the power of the ordinary collator*

Since the reservation is the withdrawal of a benefice from the power of the ordinary collator, it is important to know just how long this withdrawal endures. This question may be illustrated by the following example. The case is one which concerns a permanently conferred benefice the incumbent of which died in Rome on October 1, 1941. It is evident that the Holy See alone can validly fill that particular vacancy. But what of the next vacancy to occur, say for example that the same benefice should become vacant in the year 1949? Would this provision also belong to the Holy See, or did the benefice automatically revert to the ordinary collator after the Apostolic See had made the first appointment? The Code in no way answers this query and therefore the solution must be sought in the previous legislation or in canonical jurisprudence.

Most authors devote some consideration to this aspect of the reserved benefice. Invariably this treatment is found in their comparison between the reservation and what was termed the *affectio beneficii.* The *affectio,* often termed the tacit reservation, was any positive act whereby the Roman Pontiff manifested his intention of removing a particular benefice from the power of the ordinary collator.[67] The reader's attention was always called

[65] Canon 1421 mentions these methods.

[66] Canon 20: "Si certa de re desit expressum praescriptum legis sive generalis sive particularis, norma sumenda est, nisi agatur de poenis applicandis, a legibus latis in similibus..."

[67] Wernz, *Ius decretalium,* II, p. 454, n. 333.

to the fact that the *affectio* withdrew the benefice in question from the power of the ordinary collator only for the first vacancy to occur (*pro prima vice*). But on the corresponding question concerning the duration of the withdrawal of a reserved benefice there was a marked divergence of opinion.

The first school emphasized the permanency of the reservation of the benefice, so much so that once a benefice was reserved, all future acts whereby it was conferred upon anyone pertained to the Holy See.[68] Opposed to this interpretation is the opinion of those canonists who maintain that a reserved benefice ceases to be reserved as soon as the Holy See confers that benefice.[69] Other than the weighty extrinsic authority which supports the first of these opinions, there is little which can be said in its favor. Certainly the theme which permeates so much of the literature on reserved benefices, namely, " beneficium semel reservatum, semper remanet reservatum," cannot be adduced as a proof of the absolute permanency of the reserved benefice. That phrase is but an attempt to summarize the canonical interpretation given

[68] Reiffenstuel, *Ius canonicum,* lib. III, tit. V, n. 411: "Secundo differunt; quia beneficium reservatum nunquam amplius potest conferri ab inferiore; beneficium affectum vero, licet pro ea vice, qua Pontifex manum apposuit super eius provisione, nequeat ab inferiore aliquo conferri; potest tamen ita conferri pro alia vice, postquam provisio Papae suum effectum consecuta fuit. Unde affectio non adimit inferiori potestatem conferendi in perpetuum sed solum pro una vice; bene tamen reservatio nisi revocetur."

Soglia, *Institutiones iuris ecclesiastici publici et privati* (2 vols., Neapoli, 1864), II, 177: "Praeterea reservatio habet effectum successivum, ita ut beneficium reservatum ab inferiore collatore concedi amplius nequeat; affectio autem pro una tantum et prima vice beneficium Pontifici addicit . . ."

Schmalzgrueber, *Ius ecclesiasticum universum,* lib. III, tit. V, n. 210; Wernz, *loc. cit.*

[69] Lotterius, *De re beneficiali,* lib. I, q. XXVIII, n. 203: ". . . cum reservatio non tollatur, nisi per Papae provisionem." Lib. II, q. XX, n. 69: ". . . siquidem reservatio vel affectio perpetuo durat, donec per novam provisionem consumpta fit . . ."

Gonzalez, *De reservatione mensium,* gloss XV, 2, n. 31: "Nono quaero quando expiret ac cessat vacatio ad effectum, ut cesset reservatio? Dic quod per provisionem Papae, quamvis possessio capta non fuerit." Riganti, In regul. I, sectio I, nn. 76, 119.

by Paul II in 1467 in his constitution, *Ad Romani,*[70] and later repeated and clarified in the eleventh rule of the Chancery Rules. Now, both of these documents clearly state that the reserved benefices are to be conferred by the Roman Pontiff only the first time they become vacant.[71] Furthermore Rota decisions frequently shared the contrary view of Riganti, Lotterius, and Gonzalez.[72]

Though from the purely canonical standpoint the second school is the one to follow, it does admit one noticeable and important exception. There is one type of reserved benefice which, for all practical purposes, once it is reserved always remains withdrawn from the ordinary collator. This explains why so many of the more recent authors assert that some reserved benefices are withdrawn from the ordinary collators temporarily, while others are withdrawn permanently.[73] D'Annibale explains this doctrine quite well. First he recalls the standard threefold division of

[70] C. 14, *De praebendis et dignitatibus,* III, 2, in Extravag. com.

[71] *Ad Romani*: "... per huiusmodi reservationem et decretum remansisse et remanere semper affecta, nullumque de illis, quam primum vacare contigerit, praeter R. Pontificem *ea vice* quovis modo disponere potuisse..."

Regula Undecima: "... remansisse ac remanere per huiusmodi reservationem ac decretum affecta, nullumque de illis praeter Romanum Ponticem *ea vice* se intromittere vel disponere potuisse, sive posse quoquomodo."

[72] *Sacrae Romanae Rotae decisiones recentiores* (ed. by Farinacius, Rubeus et Campagnus, 25 vols., Venetiis, 1697), pars V, tom. I, decisio 196, n. 14: (Speaking of a benefice which was reserved because it was held by a member of the papal household) "... quod ex quo semel Papa manus apposuit per reservationem non potest inferior collator de huiusmodi beneficiis disponere, donce Papa semel disposuerit."; Pars XIX, tom. II, decisio 549, n. 6; *Sacrae Romanae Rotae Decisiones Nuperrimae* (10 vols., pro annis 1684-1706, Romae, n. d.), vol. V a, decisio 262: (Speaking of a benefice which was reserved because it had become vacant *apud Sedem*) "... vacaret apud Sedem Apostolicam, nullusque de illa praeter Summum Pontificem pro *hac vice* disponere posset."; Vol. VIII, decisio 140, n. 9.

[73] D'Annibale, *Summula theologiae moralis,* III, 35; Bouix, *De parocho,* p. 314; Sipos, *Enchiridion iuris canonici,* p. 736; Pistocchi, *De re beneficiali,* p. 189.

reserved benefices—1) *Reservatio realis* which reserves a benefice because of some element proper to the benefice itself, e. g., the reservation of episcopal sees; 2) Penal reservation; and 3) That reservation which affects a benefice either because of some characteristic of the incumbent, e. g., because he belongs to the papal household, or because of the time or place in which the benefice becomes vacant, e. g., the beneficiary dies in Rome. D'Annibale maintains that a benefice which is reserved through the reservations mentioned under the second and third classes above ceases to be reserved as soon as the Holy See confers that benefice. This has significant connotations under the present law of the Church, for most of the reservations of the Code belong to one of these two classes. Hence whenever a benefice is reserved by such a prescription, it returns to the power of the ordinary collator as soon as the Pope confers it. In discussing the first type of reservation mentioned above, i. e., the *reservatio realis*, D'Annibale asserts that such a reservation perpetually removes the benefice from the power of the local ordinary.[74]

How can this idea of the perpetuity of the withdrawal of a benefice which has been reserved by a *reservatio realis* be reconciled with the accurate juridical concept advanced by Riganti, Lotterius, and Gonzalaz as well as by numerous Rota decisions? It is really quite easy to harmonize these two schools. One may propose for example the *reservatio realis* which involves the reservation of an episcopal see. Theoretically it is correct to hold that as soon as the Pope confers the episcopal see, it is free from the limitations of the reservation. Immediately, however, a new reservation comes into being, because identically the same condition which brought about the first reservation (namely the nature of the benefice) is once more verified.

[74] It is to be noted that there are only two *reservationes reales* in the Code: the reservation of consistorial benefices and the reservation of dignities in cathedral and collegiate churches.

ARTICLE 4. THE PRESCRIPTION OF A RESERVED BENEFICE

At times it may happen that due to an oversight or some similar cause a local Ordinary will appoint a cleric to a reserved benefice. Such an appointment is, of course, invalid. Fortunately this invalidity is not necessarily permanent. The cleric invalidly appointed to a reserved benefice can and often will obtain a valid title to the benefice by legitimate prescription. Canon 1446 sets forth the essential requisites for the obtaining of a valid claim to the possession of a benefice through the agency of legitimate prescription. This canon rules that a cleric who possesses a benefice obtains that benefice by legitimate prescription if he should prove that he has been in peaceful possession of that benefice for three years in good faith, even perchance with an invalid title, provided it is not a question of simony.

This present law of the Church is a somewhat modified reenactment of the pre-Code law.[75] It certainly embodies one change from the old law and possibly a second. The possible alteration concerns the possession of good faith in the one acquiring the benefice by prescription. Under the old law it was not clear whether good faith was to be deemed a necessary requisite or not.[76] The Code is most definite in its demand that the matter of good faith be verified for the entire three years of prescription.[77] It does, however, prescind from the subjective attitude of the incumbent of the benefice once he has completed the three years' possession. Thus, if one has been in possession of a benefice in good faith for three years and then realizes that the original act of conferment was invalid, such a one may rest free of all misgivings, for he has already obtained the benefice by

[75] Formerly the *Triennalis possessio* was the thirty-sixth Chancery rule. Its purpose was primarily to safeguard the incumbent of the benefice from judicial attacks on his possession.

[76] Riganti, In regul. XXXVI, nn. 210 sq.; D'Annibale, *Summula theologiae moralis,* III, 54, ftns. 10, 11.

[77] Canon 1512.

means of legitimate prescription and enjoys both the valid and licit possession of the same.[78]

What is certainly a modification of the old law is the new ruling concerning the title of possession necessary for prescription. The Code is consistent with the thirty-sixth rule of the Chancery when it insists that the one acquiring the benefice by prescription have some title to it, even though it is invalid.[79] Without some title of possession the prescription of a benefice is simply impossible. The title itself may be invalid either because of a lack in the observance of the form required for the conferring of the benefice or because of the insufficiency of authority in the one conferring the benefice.[80] The latter deficiency is of concern to this work, for that is precisely the legal defect which obtains when the local Ordinary confers a reserved benefice.

Though the absolute necessity of at least an invalid title to the benefice has been emphasized, one must not conclude that any and every invalid title whatsoever is sufficient for obtaining a benefice by way of legal prescription. Under the pre-Code law there were two types of titles which were considered to be unsuited for the acquisition of a benefice through legal prescription. The first title was that which resulted from a transaction tainted with simony. The second was the title bestowed by a local Ordinary when he conferred a benefice reserved to the Holy See because its incumbent had died at the Apostolic See.[81] The Code has altered this rule. Now, as canon 1446 states, there is only

[78] Blat, *Commentarium textus iuris canonici*, III^2, 430; Riganti In regul. XXXVI, n. 171.

[79] Canon 1509: "Praescriptioni obnoxia non sunt: n. 6—Beneficium ecclesiasticum sine titulo." Cf. also c. 1446.

[80] Pistocchi, *De re beneficiali*, p. 237.

[81] *Sacrae Romanae Rotae decisiones nuperrimae*, Vol. VII, decisio 124, *Conchen. praestimonii*, 12 iun., 1701, n. 6: "...ad effectus regulae sufficeret quicumque titulus, quia omnis titulus dicitur coloratus, dummodo non fit de duobus exceptis in regula, nempe simoniacus, vel de reservato reservatione clausa in corpore iuris (i. e., when the beneficiary died *apud Sedem Apostolicam*)."

one type of invalid title which will not suffice for the obtaining of an ecclesiastical benefice by legal prescription, i. e., the title which has resulted from a transaction involving simony, so that today, whenever a local Ordinary, due to some oversight, confers a reserved benefice, the one who receives that benefice has a title of possession sufficient for the prescription of the benefice.

According to canon 1446 not only are the title and good faith necessary for the obtaining of the reserved benefice through prescription, but also a third requirement, namely, three years of peaceful possession of the benefice. In computing this period of time the first day of possession is not counted.[82] Thus if one took possession on July 12, 1942, the three years would not be completed until the midnight of July 12, 1945. The possession of the benefice is considered peaceful as long as it is not interrupted by judicial or extrajudicial procedure.[83] This judicial interruption commences with the legitimate citation.[84] An extrajudicial disturbance is any extrajudicial act whereby the cleric is deprived either of the possession or of the fruits of the benefice.[85]

[82] Canon 34, § 3, n. 3.

[83] Lotterius, *De re beneficiaria*, lib. II, q. LIII, n. 20; Blat, *op. cit.*, III, 430.

[84] Canon 1725, n. 4: "(Cum citatio legitime peracta fuerit . . .) Interrumpitur praescriptio, nisi aliud cautum sit ad normam can. 1508."

[85] Riganti, In regul. XXXVI, n. 61.

CHAPTER IX

BeneficES Reserved in the Code

Can. 1435. § 1. **Praeter omnia beneficia consistorialia et omnes dignitates ecclesiarum cathedralium et collegiatarum ad norman can. 396, § 1, sunt reservata Sedi Apostolicae, quanquam vacanti, sola beneficia quae infra memorantur:**

1°. Omnia beneficia, etiam curata, quae vacaverint per obitum, promotionem, renuntiationem vel translationem S. R. E. Cardinalium, Legatorum Romani Pontificis, officialium maiorum Sacrarum Congregationum, Tribunalium et Officiorum Romanae Curiae et Familiarium, etiam honoris tantum, Summi Pontificis tempore vacationis beneficii;

2°. Quae, fundata extra Romanam Curiam, vacaverint per beneficiarii obitum in ipsa Urbe;

3°. Quae invalide ob simoniae vitium collata fuerint;

4°. Denique beneficia quibus Romanus Pontifex per se vel per delegatum manus apposuit his qui sequuntur modis: si electionem ad beneficium irritam declaraverit, vel vetuerit electores ad electionem procedere; si renuntiationem admiserit; si beneficiarium promoverit, transtulerit, beneficio privaverit; si beneficium in commendam dederit.

The latter half of the nineteenth century witnessed an appeal addressed to the papacy by many members of the hierarchy urging a complete revision of the laws of the Church.[1] One of the basic reasons motivating this request was the fact that the laws of the Church were to be found in so many different sources that their study was rendered most difficult. A survey would have shown that this complaint was verified in the particular field of reserved benefices. As mentioned in the historical section, the reservations were contained not only in the *Regulae Cancellariae*,

[1] *Codex iuris canonici* (Gasparri editio), pp. xxviii, xxix.

but also in a large sampling of papal constitutions issued over a period of several centuries.

The Code has certainly remedied this situation with regard to the reservation of benefices. With remarkable conciseness it enumerates in a single canon all the benefices reserved by the present law of the Church. The Code is most explicit in pointing out that no benefices are now to be considered reserved unless they are specifically mentioned in canon 1435.[2] Since many of the former reservations, e. g., the *Regula mensium,* are not enumerated in canon 1435 and are therefore abrogated, this canon is by no means a repetition of the pre-Code law. Rather it represents an extensive revision of the entire field of reserved benefices.

The various types of reserved benefices mentioned by the Code are as follows:

a. *Consistorial benefices*

Canon 1411 states that consistorial benefices are those which are customarily conferred in consistory.[3] Maroto explains that it would be more accurate to describe them as benefices which *were* customarily conferred in consistory because at the present time most of these provisions are made not in consistory but by the Consistorial Congregation.[4] Blat shares this view adding the fact that they are merely published in consistory.[5] Though the Code mentions but two types of benefices which are conferred in consistory, namely, the cardinalate and the archbishopric,[6] all authors agree that there are many more types of consistorial benefices. As the determining factor Coronata states that a benefice is to be considered consistorial if it has any episcopal power attached to it, even though the cleric to whom it is con-

[2] Canon 1435: " . . . sunt reservata . . . *sola benefica* quae infra memorantur."

[3] Canon 1411, n. 1: "Consistorialia, quae in Consistorio conferri solent."

[4] P. Maroto, "Normae servandae ab Ordinariis"—*Apollinaris,* IV (1931), 50-54, in particular p. 52.

[5] *Commentarium textus Codicis iuris canonici,* III, 383.

[6] Canons 233, § 1 and 275.

ferred is not a bishop.[7] Thus he identifies the consistorial benefice with what the old law termed the major benefice. Cappello, Sipos, and Maroto agree with this view.[8] This means that the following clerics possess consistorial benefices: cardinals, patriarchs, primates, archbishops, bishops, prelates and abbots *nullius*, vicars and prefects apostolic, and apostolic administrators.

b. *Dignities in cathedral and collegiate chapters*

The Code describes a chapter as a college of clerics instituted for the more solemn worship of God in a particular church.[9] If the chapter is established in a cathedral church, it is called a cathedral chapter and has the added responsibility of acting as the bishop's council. If the chapter is founded in any other church, it is simply called a collegiate chapter. This latter type is found more frequently in Italy and Spain.[10] The cathedral chapter is characteristic of most countries in which the Church has advanced beyond the missionary stage. No chapters, however, are found in the United States and therefore this reservation of the dignities in them assumes no practical importance for this country.

Every chapter has a number of offices which are to be conferred on the clerics constituting the chapter. Not all of these are reserved to the Apostolic See. The only ones reserved are those which are known as dignities. The general norm to determine whether a given office is a dignity is to see if it has some prerogative of honor attached to it.[11] The practical norm for this determination will usually be found in the statutes of the

[7] Coronata, *Institutiones iuris canonici*, II, 362.

[8] Cappello, *Summa iuris canonici*, II, 472, n. 863; Sipos, *Enchiridion iuris canonici*, p. 726; Maroto, "Normae servandae ab Ordinariis"—*Apollinaris*, IV (1931), 52.

[9] Canon 391, § 1.

[10] Vermeersch-Creusen, *Epitome iuris canonici*, I, 362.

[11] Chelodi-Bertagnolli, *Ius de personis iuxta Codicem iuris canonici* (Tridenti: edit. Tridentum, 1927), p. 340; Vermeersch-Creusen, *Epitome*, I, 367.

chapter because ordinarily these statutes will definitely state which offices are to be considered dignities.[12] There is no precept in the Code regulating the number or the names of the dignities. Ordinarily the number of dignities in any chapter will range from one to seven.[13] The titles which commonly designate the dignities in a chapter are as follows: *decanus, praepositus, archdiaconus, archipresbyter, primicerius, custos, praecentor, scholasticus, cantor,* and *thesaurarius.*

The present law states that every dignity in cathedral and collegiate chapters is reserved to the Roman Pontiff. This represents a considerable amplification of the corresponding pre-Code reservation, which affected only the *principal* dignity in the chapter and indeed only that principal dignity which had an annual income in excess of ten gold florins.[14] Today all the dignities are reserved to the Pope. There are no exceptions, not even those dignities which have no prebends or income attached to them.[15] Both Vermeersch-Creusen and Chelodi expressed the opinion that those who prior to the Code had the apostolic privilege of conferring dignities could continue to confer these dignities after the promulgation of the Code.[16] D'Angelo adopted the contrary stand.[17] Just recently the Sacred Congregation of the Council shared this negative view, stating that canon 1435, § 1, has abrogated all apostolic privileges concerning the bestowal of dignities.[18]

[12] Ayrinhac, *Constitution of the Church in the new Code of canon law* (New York: Longmans, Green, 1930), p. 236.

[13] Coronata, *op. cit.*, I, 515.

[14] Regula IV Cancellariae Apostolicae.

[15] Commissio Pontificia Interpretationis, 1 iul., 1922—*AAS,* XIV (1922), 408; Bouscaren, *Canon law digest,* I, 218.

[16] Vermeersch-Creusen, *Epitome,* I, 368; Chelodi-Bertagnolli, *Ius de personis,* p. 343.

[17] "De collatione dignitatum"—*Apollinaris,* III (1930), 322-325, esp. p. 322.

[18] *AAS,* XXXIII (1941), 72: "Verum etsi in casu ageretur de apostolico privilegio, abrogatum hoc fuisse videtur praesertim per canonem 1435, § 1, generatim statuentem, omnes dignitates . . ."

c. *All benefices, even those to which the care of souls is attached which become vacant through the death, promotion, resignation, or transfer of* (1) *cardinals of the Holy Roman Church,* (2) *legates of the Roman Pontiff,* (3) *major officials of the Sacred Congregations, Tribunals, and Offices of the Roman Curia, and* (4) *members of the household, even honorary members, of the Supreme Pontiff at the time of the vacancy of the benefice.*

Before discussing the four types of reserved benefices mentioned in this section of canon 1435 one may well recall that canon 1413 supplies the presumption that any given canon in this section of the Code is concerned only with non-consistorial benefices.[19] Since there is nothing in this or in the following three numbers of paragraph one of canon 1435 to destroy this presumption,[20] all of the reservations mentioned from now on do not affect consistorial benefices. Such a distinction may seem useless in view of the fact, that, as mentioned previously, all consistorial benefices are reserved to the Pope. Yet the reservation of consistorial benefices is not so absolute as to exclude all exceptions. Thus until the year 1934 the suffragan sees of Gurk, Lavant, and Seckau were exempt from the reservation of consistorial benefices and could be freely conferred by the Archbishop of Salzburg in Austria.[21] Therefore if one of these suffragan bishops had died in Rome prior to the Concordat of 1934, the conferring of his vacant see would not have been reserved to the Roman Pontiff. The continued status of non-reservation would have obtained precisely in view of the legal presumption enunciated in canon 1413, namely, the norm of canon 1435 does not apply to consistorial benefices. This regulation of the present law coincides with the accepted pre-Code interpretation.[22]

[19] Canon 1413, § 1: "Nisi aliud appareat, canones qui sequuntur, de beneficiis tantum non consistorialibus proprie dictis intelligi debent."

[20] Linden, *Der Tod des benefiziaten in Rom*, p. 242.

[21] Maroto, *Institutiones iuris canonici ad normam novi Codicis* (2 vols., Tom. I, 3rd ed., Romae: Apud Commentarium pro Religiosis, 1921), I, 689, footnote 1. This privilege was abrogated by the Concordat of 1934. Cf. Perugini, *Concordata vigentia* (Romae: Apollinaris, 1934), pp. 266-270.

[22] Cf. chapter III, article II, of the historical section.

In the discussion on the reserved benefices mentioned in this section it is important to note that such benefices are reserved only if they become vacant in one of four ways, i. e., by death, by promotion, by resignation (when it has been accepted), or by transfer. If the benefice becomes vacant in any other manner, it is not reserved.[23] Thus if the local Ordinary removes a member of the papal household from his perpetual benefice, that benefice is not reserved.

One is to be regarded as a legate of the Roman Pontiff if he is sent either as a legate *a latere*, as a nuncio or internuncio, or as an Apostolic delegate.[24] The phrase, "major officials of the Roman Curia," is a technical expression which embraces all the more important personnel of the curia.[25] The *Ordo Servandus* of Pope Pius X clearly indicates the major officials of each of the Sacred Congregations of the Roman Curia.[26] The canonists summarize the teaching of this enactment by stating that the major officials of the Congregations are the prefect, secretaries, and subsecretaries. When the Pope is the prefect of the Congregation, an assessor is added as a major official.[27] Practically the same general schema of major officials exists in the tribunals and offices of the Roman Curia with the exception of the Rota, the major officials of which are the ten auditors, the promoter of justice, and the defender of the bond.[28]

[23] Blat, *Commentarium textus Codicis iuris canonici*, III[2], 418.

[24] Canons 266-268.

[25] *Ordo servandus in Sacris Congregationibus, Tribunalibus, Officiis Romanae Curiae: Pars Prima, Normae communes*, 29 iun., 1908, cap. I, 1°, et cap. II, 1°—*AAS*, I (1909), 36-37.

[26] *Pars Altera: Normae Peculiares*, 29 sept., 1908, cap. VII—*AAS*, I (1909), 78 sq.

[27] Vermeersch-Creusen, *Epitome iuris canonici*, I, 302; Ayrinhac, *Constitution of the Church*, p. 55.

[28] For a complete list of the officials of the tribunals and offices the reader may consult Cappello, *De curia romana iuxta reformationem a Pio X sapientissime inductam* (2 vols., Romae, 1911-1912), I, 386, 454, 465, 468, 470, 471.

Consideration will now be given to the final class of clerics, i. e., the members of the papal household, whose benefices are reserved when they become vacant through death, resignation, promotion, or transfer. This phase is of extreme importance in this country because of the large number of American clerics who are members of the papal household. The several hundred resident clerics of this country who are members of the papal household have received this title not because of any personal service they render the Pope, but simply because the Holy Father has bestowed this title on them as an *honor.* Yet honorary membership, as canon 1435 explicitly states, is sufficient for this reservation to take effect.

It will be found that the clerics here in the United States who are members of the papal household belong to one of three classes: prothonotaries Apostolic *ad instar,* domestic prelates, and papal chamberlains.[29] One who belongs to either of the first two classes is formally addressed as the right reverend monsignor; one who belongs to the third class is addressed as the very reverend monsignor. Before explaining the difference between the first two classes of honorary membership in the papal household and the third class (papal chamberlains), it is important to repeat that all three classes are members of the papal household and hence the benefices held even by the papal chamberlains are subject to this reservation. The difference consists in this that the honor bestowed on the papal chamberlains is only temporary, i. e., they are members of the household only for the duration of the reign of the Pope who promoted them to this honor. Thus with the death or resignation of this Pontiff, they cease to be papal chamberlains.[30]

29 "Papal reservation of appointment to parishes"—*The Ecclesiastical Review,* LXXXIX (1933), 433.

30 Nainfa, *Costume of prelates of the Catholic Church* (2nd ed., Baltimore, 1926), pp. 24-87; Rossi, *De paroecia iuxta Codicem iuris canonici* (Romae: Pustet, 1923), p. 140, ftn. b; Cavigioli, *Manuale di diritto canonico* (Torino: Società editrice internazionale, 1934), p. 502.

It will be noted that the Code is concerned only with the benefices of those clerics who are members of the papal household at the time when their benefices become vacant.[31] This is the sense in which most canonists have interpreted the phrase "tempore vacationis beneficii."[32] Thus if an American cleric had been made a papal chamberlain by Pius XI and died not during the reign of Pius XII, his benefice would not be reserved unless the present Pope had also made him a member of the papal household. The reason for this is that he ceased to be a member of the household the very moment Pius XI died.[33] Again, if a priest is made a monsignor after he has resigned his benefice, but at a time when the benefice which he resigned is still vacant, that benefice would not be reserved.

Does this limitation which is imposed by the phrase "tempore vacationis" on the members of the papal household apply also to the other dignitaries and officials mentioned in canon 1435, § 1, 1°, i. e., to the cardinals, legates and major officials of the curia? In other words, will the benefice of a cardinal be reserved only on the condition that the cleric is a cardinal at the moment the benefice becomes vacant? Those who have treated this problem

[31] Canon 1435, § 1, n. 1: "Omnia beneficia . . . Familiarium, etiam honoris tantum, Summi Pontificis *tempore vacationis beneficii.*"

[32] Pistocchi, *de re beneficiali*, p. 185; Blat, *op. cit.*, III[2], 419; Coronata, *Institutiones iuris canonici*, II, 386; Rossi, *op. cit.*, p. 140; Hilling, "Was bedeutet der Zusatz 'tempore vacationis beneficii' in can. 1435, § 1, n. 1 CJC?"—*AKKR*, CIV (1924), 282-287; Stephanus Sipos, "Quid significent verba 'temporis vacationis beneficii" in can. 1435, § 1, n. 1 CJC?"—*AKKR*, CVI (1926), 575-576; Vermeersch, "De verbis can. 1435, § 1, 'tempore vacationis beneficii'"—*Periodica*, XXI (1932), 160*-161*.

[33] Prümmer presents an entirely different interpretation of the phrase "tempore vacationis beneficii." With some hesitation he states that it may indicate that the Pope has the power to confer such benefices by the *ius concursus*—Prümmer, *Manuale iuris canonici* (5th ed., Friburgi Brisgoviae: Herder Co., 1927), q. 430. This view is strongly criticised in the three magazine articles mentioned in the preceding footnote, and rightly so. Canon 1435 states that it is treating of reserved benefices. Now, there is an essential difference between the *ius concursus* and the *ius reservationis*, as has been pointed out in article four of chapter two.

hold that the benefices will be reserved only if the clerics were cardinals, legates, or major officials at the very moment when their benefices become vacant. Hilling bases this conclusion on the contention that the phrase "*tempore vacationis beneficii*" is to be referred not only to the members of the papal household but also to the other clerics mentioned in this canon.[34] Sipos and Vermeersch admit Hilling's conclusion but deny his line of reasoning.[35] They maintain that if the phrase "*tempore vacationis beneficii*" were to modify all the members mentioned in this section of canon 1435, there would be a comma placed after the word, "*Pontificis.*" The more one studies the structure of this canon, the more one will agree with this remark on the punctuation. Vermeersch and Sipos arrive at the same conclusion as that reached by Hilling in the following manner. Canon 1435 reserves the benefices which become vacant by death, promotion, transfer, or resignation of cardinals. Now if a cleric who had been a cardinal but for some reason or other had lost that dignity should die, it is obvious that the conditions set down in the canon would not be verified and hence the benefice held by that cleric would not be reserved. In this case, they maintain, the benefice would not become vacant by the death of a cardinal but rather by the death of a cleric who had been a cardinal.

d. *Benefices located outside the Roman Curia which become vacant through the death of the beneficiary in the City itself*

This represents a modified version of the first general reservation, the *Licet ecclesiarum*. Under the present law two conditions must be verified before the reservation becomes effective: First, the benefice in question must be located outside the Roman Curia (*fundata extra Romanam Curiam*). Secondly, the cleric

[34] Hilling, "Was bedeutet der Zusatz 'tempore vacationis beneficii' in can. 1435, § 1, n. 1, CJC?"—*AKKR*, CIV (1924), 286.

[35] Sipos, "Quid significent verba 'tempore vacationis beneficii' in can. 1435, § 1, n. 1 CJC?"—*AKKR*, CVI (1926), 576; Vermeersch, "De verbis can. 1435, § 1, 'tempore vacationis beneficii'"—*Periodica*, XXI (1932), 161'.

possessing that benefice must die within the City itself (*in ipsa Urbe*).

The authors are not in complete accord concerning the extent of the territory which is outside the Roman Curia. All but one, however, conceive it as a territory which does not change or vary. The one exception in this regard is Blat. First he maintains that the territory embraced by this terminology depends on the actual residence of the Roman Pontiff and his curia.[36] Thus if the Pope and his curia were to reside in the city of Naples, Blat would consider that city as marking the location of the Roman Curia. Though one may invoke a strong counter-argument in favor of the opposite view, yet the law furnishes no direct text to disprove this contention of Blat. Unfortunately, however, Blat continued and stated that any place which is situated within two days' journey of the Roman Curia is considered within the Roman Curia. He is evidently confusing the present reservation of the Code with the former reservation contained in the decretal *Praesenti* (1298) of Boniface VIII, whereby any benefice which became vacant through the death of its incumbent within two days' journey of the Roman Curia was reserved.[37] That reservation was distinct from the *Licet ecclesiarum* and was not renewed in the Code. Therefore it is no longer in force.[38] Prior to the Code when the Apostolic datary conferred such reserved benefices, they were always designated as *vacantia intra duas dietas legales* and never as *vacantia apud curiam*.[39]

Pistocchi, Linden, Rossi and Augustine interpret the phrase, "*fundata extra Romanam Curiam*," as indicative of a definite territory which in no way depends on the actual presence of the Roman Pontiff and his curia. The first of these authors contends that it means any benefice located in any diocese other than the

[36] Blat, *Commentarium textus Codicis iuris canonici*, III², 419.

[37] C. 34, *De praebendis et dignitatibus*, III, 4, in VI°.

[38] Cocchi, *Commentarium in Codicem iuris canonici*, III, 244; Pistocchi, *op. cit.*, p. 187.

[39] Riganti, in regul. VIII, sectio I, n. 156.

diocese of Rome.[40] The others hold that it means any benefice which exists outside the City of Rome.[41] The latter opinion seems to be the better one in view of an indirect argument afforded by canon 238. This canon rules that the cardinals are not to depart from the curia without the permission of the Roman Pontiff. Then the canon states that those cardinals who are not bound to reside in the curia need the Pope's permision to leave the City of Rome whenever they come there. Thus it seems likely that the Code is using the two terms, "Curia" and "Urbem" synonymously.[42]

The second essential requirement for this reservation is that the beneficiary die in the city itself. This implies a significant change in the law. Before the Code the reservation affected benefices which became vacant *apud curiam.* Since the curia at times departed from Rome in the performance of its duties, this reservation was capable of affecting benefices the incumbents of which died outside Rome. The Code removes such a possibility by stating that it is concerned solely with those benefices which become vacant by the death of their incumbents in the City itself. The expression "in ipsa Urbe" means the City of Rome.[43] Thus, if the Holy Father and his curia were to reside in some city other than Rome, the present law would not reserve the benefices of those clerics who died in that city. Cappello is the only commentator to contradict this view.[44] He interprets this particular point as though it were nothing but a repetition of the pre-Code

[40] Pistocchi, *De re beneficiali*, p. 187.

[41] Linden, *op. cit.*, p. 246; Rossi, *De paroecia*, p. 141; Augustine, *A commentary on the new Code of canon law*, VI, 518.

[42] Linden, *op. cit.*, p. 246.

[43] Fanfani, *De iure parochorum*, p. 97, footnote 1; Pistocchi, *op. cit.*, p. 187; John Coady, *The appointment of pastors* (Catholic University of America Canon Law Studies, n. 52, Washington, D. C.: Catholic University of America, 1929), p. 102.

[44] Cappello, *Summa iuris canonici*, II, 487: "Nomine Urbis venit non solum Roma, sed quaelibet urbs ubi actu commoretur Papa cum sua Curia."

law, which reserved those benefices becoming vacant *apud curiam.* In view of the new terminology employed by the Code, viz., *beneficia vacantia in ipsa Urbe,* his opinion seems untenable.

Prümmer and Rossi assert that this prescription of the Code does not reserve the benefices of all the clerics who die in Rome but only the benefices of those clerics who are in Rome because of ecclesiastical business. In their estimation, if a cleric dies in Rome while there on a pilgrimage or on a sight-seeing tour, his benefice is not reserved.[45] Neither of these authors adduces any proof for this contention. It is especially significant that they do not refer to any of the older authors who wrote so extensively and thoroughly on reserved benefices. The writer has never noted any such distinction in any of the standard pre-Code works on reserved benefices. In view of this utter lack of proof the opinion should be regarded as erroneous. The Code certainly supplies no ground for such a distinction. The same is equally true of the old legislation.[46] Furthermore this erroneous view has been rejected by many of the canonists who have studied this point.[57] Finally, and of the greatest importance in disproving such an opinion, is the fact that it is the practice of the Roman Curia to regard as reserved the benefice of any cleric who dies in Rome, independent of the reason of his presence there.[48]

e. *Those benefices which have been invalidly conferred because of simony*

Some authors simply state that this is a penal reservation.[49] It is with some hesitation that one should admit such a classifica-

[45] Prümmer, *Manuale iuris canonici* (6th ed., Friburgi Brisgoviae: Herder, 1933), p. 515; Rossi, *De paroecia,* p. 135, ftn. 10.

[46] Linden, *op. cit.,* p. 257.

[47] Linden, *op. cit.,* pp. 256, 257; Vermeersch-Creusen, *Epitome iuris canonici,* II, 540; Pistocchi, op. cit., p. 187; Beste, *Introductio in Codicem,* p. 708; Blat. *op. cit.,* III, 419; Bouuaert-Simenon, *Manuale iuris canonici,* p. 587, n. 963.

[48] Linden, *op. cit.,* p. 256.

[49] Coronata, *Institutiones iuris canonici,* II, 386; Pistocchi, *De re beneficiali,* p. 188; Sipos, *Enchiridion iuris canonici,* p. 737, ftn. 11.

tion for this reservation. In the strict meaning of the term this reservation does not always constitute a penalty. As has been previously mentioned, the reservation withdraws the right of conferring the benefice from the one who ordinarily makes this provision. Now in some cases in which simony is involved, the ordinary collator will be completely innocent of any wrong. More accurate, then, is the stand of Blat and Cocchi, who classify this reservation as one *ad instar poenae*.[50]

The question of simony itself is a purely incidental consideration in this work. Consequently a detailed treatment of its nature is beyond the scope of this thesis. For the precise concept of simony the reader may consult any of the commentators who have written on this point.[51]

It is important to realize that the Code does not reserve all benefices which have been conferred by a transaction involving simony. Canon 1435 states explicitly that this reservation affects only those benefices which have been *invalidly* conferred because of the fault of simony. This, of course, presupposes that there can be occasions when a benefice is validly conferred even though the provision is tainted with simony. Canon 729 verifies this inference. This canon enacts the general norm that, whenever a benefice is conferred through a simoniacal transaction, the benefice is conferred invalidly. Then it immediately adds two exceptions to this sanction of invalidity, namely, when the simony has been placed to injure the one receiving the benefice or when the cleric receiving the benefice protests against the simony. An example of the first exception would be had if someone commits the simony imagining that he will thereby render the appointee ineligible for the benefice. In either of these two cases, then, the simony does not invalidate the conferring of the benefice and hence the benefice is not reserved to the Roman Pontiff.

[50] Blat, *Commentarium textus Codicis iuris canonici*, III², 420; Cocchi, *Commentarium in Codicem iuris canonici*, III, 244.

[51] Ryder, *Simony* (Catholic University of America, Canon Law Studies, n. 65, Washington, D. C., 1931) gives an extensive bibliography.

Thus it is evident that the principle stated in canon 729 will determine those benefices which are reserved by canon 1435. Now, canon 729 speaks simply of simony and thus in the lack of any acompanying distinction comprises simony whether it offends against the divine law or merely against the ecclesiastical law.[52] Cappello makes the practical observation that it is the former type of simony which is more likely to occasion the reservation of benefices.[53] This is explained by the fact that there are so many ways by which this type of simony can be committed.[54] Nevertheless simony contrary to ecclesiastical law can also nullify the conferring of benefices and hence effect their reservation. Thus canon 1441 condemns as simoniacal all deductions from the revenue of the benefice and all compensations or payments made by the cleric in the act of provision, which accrue to the one conferring the benefice, to the patron, or to any others. Any violation of this law [55] reserves the benefice concerned to the Roman Pontiff.

This reservation does not become effective until it has been established that the simony invalidated the conferring of the benefice.[56] This means that if the simony is purely internal, i. e., if it cannot be proven or deduced from the external circumstances surrounding the provision, the benefice does not become reserved.[57]

f. *Those benefices which the Roman Pontiff either personally or through a delegate has touched in one of the following ways:* (1) *if he has declared an election null or has forbidden the electors to proceed with the election;* (2) *if he has accepted*

[52] See canon 727 for this distinction.

[53] Cappello, *Summa iuris canonici*, II, 487.

[54] Coronata, *Institutiones iuris canonici*, II, 7, 8.

[55] This canon does not forbid all types of pensions derived from the revenue of the benefice. Cf. c. 1429.

[56] Pistocchi, *op. cit.*, p. 188.

[57] Cf. canon 728 and Maroto, *Institutiones iuris canonici*, I, 785.

the resignation of the beneficiary; (3) *if he has promoted or transferred the beneficiary or deprived him of his benefice; or* (4) *if he has given the benefice in commendam.*

Here is the Code's adaptation of that canonical institution which is termed the *affectio beneficii.* In classifying these affected benefices as reserved benefices the Code has definitely abolished any real distinction between the reservation and the *affectio.*[58] In the future there can be no question of any real difference between those benefices reserved by the intervention of the Pope and the other classes of reserved benefices.

The canonists have consistently recognized that the general norm to determine whether a benefice has been reserved by the *affectio* is to see if the Pope has touched that benefice in such a manner as to manifest his intention of conferring it.[59] Thus, the reservation of the benefice was not signified on every occasion in which the Pope touched a benefice. Still Gonzalez lists twenty-three possible ways in which the *affectio* could be accomplished.[60] Most pre-Code canonists did not present such a detailed report of this point. In general they listed the same four methods which the Code has listed.[61] Under the present law, however, a benefice will not be reserved unless the Pope touches it in one of the four ways expressly mentioned in canon 1435. It is important to remember that this list in canon 1435 is all-inclusive.[62] Thus, if the Pope touches a benefice in a manner not

[58] Wernz-Vidal, *Ius canonicum,* II, 252, ftn. 28; Pistocchi, *De re beneficiali,* p. 188.

[59] Gonzalez, *De reservatione mensium,* gloss, LII, n. 38; Garcia, *De beneficiis ecclesiasticis,* pars Va, cap. I, n. 150; Reiffenstuel, *Ius canonicum universum,* lib. III, tit. V, n. 422; Schmalzgrueber, *Ius ecclesiasticum universum,* lib. III, tit. V, n. 212.

[60] *De reservatione mensium,* glossa LII, nn. 15-37.

[61] Garcia, *De beneficiis ecclesiasticis,* pars V, cap. I, nn. 138 sq.; Reiffenstuel, *Ius canonicum universum,* lib. III, tit. V, nn. 415-420; Schmalzgrueber, *op. cit.,* lib. III, tit. V, nn. 211 sq.

[62] Coronata, *Institutiones iuris canonici,* II, 386; Blat, *Commentarium,* III², 420.

mentioned in canon 1435, § 1, 4°, e. g., if he imposes a pension on a benefice, it would not bring about a reservation.

Before proceeding to explain the four ways in which the *affectio* can obtain one may well emphasize the fact that the reservation becomes effective whenever the Pope touches the benefice either personally or through a delegate. Thus, if he acts either through his curia or through an individual delegated for such a performance, the benefice will be reserved.[63] Furthermore, it makes no difference how he touches the benefice, whether it be through a formal judicial trial, through an administrative process, by a decree, or in any other manner whatever.

The first means whereby a benefice becomes affected is the declaration of the nullity of an election to that benefice or the prohibition against proceeding with the election. It makes no difference whether the one elected has accepted the election or not. The important consideration here is that the canon is speaking only of the election and not of the confirmation of the election by the proper ecclesiastical superior. Therefore, if the Pope forbids this confirmation, the benefice does not become reserved.

In the second place a benefice is reserved if the Pope accepts the resignation of the beneficiary. Under the ordinary routine of ecclesiastical affairs the Pope and his delegates accept the resignation of very few benefices.[64] Every cleric, however, can send his resignation directly to Rome. Such a procedure is more likely to occur when the local superior has refused to accept the resignation or has not acted on the proposed resignation within one month.[65]

In the third place the benefice is reserved whenever the Pope promotes or transfers the beneficiary or when he deprives the beneficiary of his benefice. A cleric is promoted when he is given a benefice of a higher order than that of his former benefice, e. g.,

[63] Blat, *Commentarium*, III, 420.

[64] Cf. canons 187 and 1484-1488, which indicate that the local Ordinaries normally accept the resignation.

[65] Cf. canon 189.

when a pastor is promoted to the episcopacy. The transfer implies a change from one benefice to another which is not of a higher order. The privation is to be understood in its usual sense, i. e., as penal privation.[66] The administrative removal of a beneficiary is privation only in the broad sense of the term [67] and hence would not reserve the benefice. The *affectio* is called the reservation *iuxta decretum* because it is the practice of the Roman Curia to state in the decree of promotion, deprivation, or transfer that the benefice is reserved to the Holy See. This is exemplified in the bulls of episcopal appointments.[68]

The fourth and final type of the *affectio* obtains whenever the Pope gives a benefice *in commendam*. A benefice is bestowed *in commendam* when the appointee is authorized by the competent ecclesiastical authority to derive from the benefice its income or revenue apart from his exercise or performance of the attached duties and obligations.[69] It is immaterial whether this concession is temporary or permanent.[70] This type of reservation, however, will occur rather seldom for, as Rossi remarks, relatively few benefices are now given *in commendam*.[71]

[66] Coronata, *Institutiones iuris canonici*, I, 321.

[67] Carl Meier, *Penal administrative procedure against negligent pastors* (Catholic University of America Canon Law Studies, n. 140, Washington, D. C.: Catholic University of America Press, 1941), p. 92.

[68] Francesco Bersani, "Le innovazioni del Codice circa il conferimento dei benefici"—*Il Monitore Ecclesiastico*, XXX (1918), 341-348, esp. p. 344.

[69] Cf. canon 1412, n. 5; Bouuaert et Simenon, *op. cit.*, p. 579.

[70] Blat, *Commentarium textus Codicis*, III^2, 420.

[71] Rossi, *De paroecia*, p. 146, footnote 34.

CHAPTER X

Benefices the Conferring of Which Has Devolved Upon the Holy See

When one is negligent in using his right to confer a benefice, that right will frequently be transferred to another ecclesiastical authority. Such a transfer of the right of conferring a benefice is termed the *devolutio beneficii.*[1]

Under the law existing before the Code the conferring of a benefice usually devolved from one ecclesiastical authority to the next higher ecclesiastical authority, e. g., from the cathedral chapter to the bishop, from the bishop to the metropolitan, etc.[2]

The Code has brought about a great change in this regard by ruling that the conferring of benefices in many cases devolves directly upon the Holy See. Thus it is that under the present law many devolved benefices can practically be considered the equivalent of reserved benefices. If any ecclesiastical superior attempts to confer a benefice the conferring of which has devolved upon the Holy See, his act stands invalid.[3] Despite this similarity in their effects the reservation and the *devolutio* represent two canonical institutions which are basically distinct.[4] The one is a withdrawal of a benefice, the other the transfer of the right of conferring a benefice. What is of extreme importance

[1] Lotterius, *De re beneficiaria,* II, q. XXIV, n. 2; Wernz-Vidal, *Ius canonicum,* II, 241.

[2] When the bishop was the collator who was originally negligent, the conferring devolved first to his chapter and only then to the metropolitan. Cf. canon 8 of the III General Lateran Council in 1179—c. 2, X, *De concessione praebendae et ecclesiae non vacantis,* III, 8.

[3] Cc. 3, 4, et 5, X, *De supplenda negligentia prelatorum,* I, 10; Leurenius, *Forum beneficiale,* III, q. 744; Coronata, *Institutiones iuris canonici,* II, 384; Wernz-Vidal, *Ius canonicum,* II, 244.

[4] Rossi, *De paroecia,* p. 147: "...quae, cum sint inter sese omnino diversae..."

is the fact that the *devolutio* affects manual benefices,[5] whereas the reservation affects them only when it expressly mentions them.

Canon 1432 sets forth the general legislation on the *devolutio beneficii.* It asserts that if the Ordinary does not confer a benefice within six months after he has received notice of its vacancy, its conferring automatically devolves upon the Holy See.[6] It does, however, safeguard those exceptions mentioned in canon 458, which are concerned with the provision of parochial benefices.

One must first note that canon 1432 refers only to those benefices the free disposal of which belongs to the Ordinary.[7] It does not directly legislate for those benefices the beneficiaries of which are nominated by a patron or elected by a group. Through the negligence of the patrons or electors, however, such benefices can become subject to the free disposal of the Ordinary and hence subject to canon 1432. Thus, if the patron should fail to present his candidate within four months, the benefice in question can at times be freely bestowed by the Ordinary.[8]

The Ordinary is allotted a period of six months in which to confer the benefices belonging to his free disposal.[9] In view of the response of the Pontifical Commission for the Authentic Interpretation of the Code on Nov. 24, 1920,[10] there can be no doubt

[5] Leurenius, *op. cit.*, III, q. 744, p. 481; Garcia, *de beneficiis*, pars V, c. III, n. 46; Gonzalez, *De reservatione mensium*, gloss. V, sectio VI, n. 55; Lotterius, lib. II, q. XXIV, n. 4.

[6] Canon 1432, § 3: "Si Ordinarius intra semestre ab habita certa vacationis notitia beneficium non contulerit, huius collatio devolvitur ad Sedem Apostolicam, salvo praescripto can. 458."

[7] Blat, *Commentarium textus Codicis iuris canonici*, III^2, 416; Wernz-Vidal, *Ius canonicum*, II, 242; Coronata, *op. cit.*, II, 384.

[8] Confer canon 161. For similar cases confer cc. 178, 182, 1458, 1465, 2391.

[9] Confer cc. 155, 1432, § 3.

[10] *AAS*, XII (1920), 577. This reply stated that the conferring of benefices did not devolve upon the Holy See when the Ordinary failed to confer it not through negligence but due to the absolute want of subjects.

that this period of time is to be computed as *tempus utile.* It commences to lapse only when the Ordinary has received notification of the vacancy of the benefice. In accordance with canon 34, § 3, n. 3, the day on which the notification is received is not computed as part of the time. Though canon 1432, § 3, speaks expressly only of such benefices as devolving upon the Holy See which have been left vacant for a period longer than six months through negligence on the part of the *Ordinary,* Coronata and Blat hold that under like circumstances the *devolutio* attaches to those benefices which in virtue of canon 1432, § 1, pertain to the free disposal of cardinal priests and cardinal deacons.[11] Such a stand, however, seems to be a misinterpretation of the Code. Canon 18 sets forth the fundamental norm of canonical interpretation, viz., that ecclesiastical laws are to be understood according to the proper signification of the words as considered in their text and context. Now the word *Ordinarius* has a specific meaning as defined in canon 198 and does not include a cardinal priest or a cardinal deacon. If the legislator had intended that the vacant benefices in the churches or titles of the cardinal priests or cardinal deacons should devolve upon the Holy See, he could—and one may reasonably suppose that he would—have included express mention of the cardinals in paragraph three as well as in paragraph one of canon 1432.

Canon 1432, § 3, expresses the general rule that the conferring of all benefices devolves upon the Apostolic See whenever the Ordinary fails to confer the benefice within six months. Canon 458, however, permits an exception in favor of the conferring of *parishes.* This canon states that a delay is admissible if in the prudent judgment of the Ordinary the circumstances of places or persons suggest a postponement. Thus the Code recognizes the prudent judgment of the Ordinary as the determining factor in this consideration.[12] The standard authors list the following cir-

[11] Coronata, *op. cit.,* II, 384; Blat, *op. cit.,* III, 416. Cf. canons 1432, § 1, and 231, 2.

[12] Fanfani, *De iure parochorum,* p. 102.

cumstances as the most likely ones which may induce the Ordinary to delay the conferring of parochial benefices: lack of suitable priests, lack of sufficient beneficial endowment, interference by the political powers, persecution, disturbance in the parish especially upon the Ordinary's removal of the former pastor, and time of war.[13]

During the First World War the Holy See withdrew the obligation of conferring parishes within six months.[14]

[13] Pistocchi, *De re beneficiali*, p. 175; Cappello, *Summa iuris canonici*, II, 26; Rossi, *De paroecia*, p. 102; Beste, *Introductio in Codicem*, p. 287.

[14] S. C. C., 26 febr. 1916—*AAS*, VIII (1916), 445.

CHAPTER XI

Benefices Which Are Exempt from the Present Reservations

Article 1. Benefices Exempt by Law

In the historical section of this treatise mention was made of the fact that there were many classes of benefices which were not affected by the reservations. The same condition is verified today as the Code exempts the following types of benefices from the reservations:

a. *Manual benefices.* It has been the constant teaching of all canonists that manual benefices were not subject to the reservation unless that reservation expressly included them. The Code admits this same exception in the second paragraph of canon 1435.[1]

The precise determination of the nature of a manual benefice, however, presents some difficulty. Most pre-Code canonists described the manual benefices as those *amovibilia ad nutum.*[2] Sometimes, though less frequently, they were simply termed *revocabilia.* This term was always understood as meaning revocable *ad nutum.*[3] The Code has adopted this latter terminology and defines the manual benefice as one which has been conferred revocably.[4] Consequently, this definition must be accepted according to its former usage, i. e., as indicative of a benefice which is revocable *ad nutum.*

[1] "At nunquam sunt reservata, nisi id expresse dicatur, beneficia manualia aut iuris patronatus laicalis vel mixti."

[2] Riganti, In regul. I, sectio I, n. 316; Lotterius, *De re beneficiaria,* lib. I, q. VII, n. 20; Scavini, *Theologia moralis universalis,* III, 523.

[3] Reiffenstuel, *Ius canonicum universum,* lib. III, tit. V, n. 42.

[4] Canon 1411, n. 4: "(beneficia ecclesiastica dicuntur) Manualia, temporaria seu amovibilia, vel perpetua seu inamovibilia, prout conferuntur *revocabiliter* vel in perpetuum."

Just what is meant when it is stated that a manual benefice is one which is revocable *ad nutum?* In its etymological sense such a phrase would denote a benefice from which the incumbent could be removed at the will or pleasure of another. It would signify a removal which could be completely arbitrary on the part of the one removing. No cause would be required, no process would be necessary. But may one reasonably conclude that this literal meaning of the phrase *amovibilia ad nutum* determines which benefices are manual? Despite the opinion of many of the earlier canonists, e. g., of Gonzalez, Garcia, Reiffenstuel, and Schmalzgrueber,[5] as Cappello notes,[6] most of the pre-Code canonists would have answered this question in the negative, because there were manual benefices in France and Belgium whose incumbents (commonly called *desservants* or *succursales*) could be validly removed only where a *just cause* was present. This opinion, which demanded the existence of a just cause for the removal of a cleric from such manual benefices, was supported as the legally accepted doctrine in many documents of the Roman Curia.[7]

Furthermore the phrase *amovibilia ad nutum* insofar as it modified the manual benefice was subject to an even more rigid interpretation. Thus under the pre-Code laws there were circumstances in which the holders of manual benefices could be removed only by means of a canonical process (not necessarily judicial). Take the situation here in the United States. Granted that at that time our missions were not benefices. Yet they were ecclesiastical offices and their rectors were in most cases removable at the will of the local Ordinary.[8] Thus they offer an opportunity to study the meaning of the phrase *amovibilia ad nutum.* In

[5] Bouix (*De parocho,* pp. 403-425) presents a detailed treatment of this entire discussion.

[6] *De administrativa amotione parochorum seu commentarium in decretum "Maxima cura"* (Romae, 1911), p. 118, footnote 2.

[7] Pierantonelli (*Praxis fori ecclesiastici* [Romae, 1883], pp. 95, 96 and 110) lists many such documents.

[8] Golden, *Parochial benefices in the new Code,* pp. 99, 100.

1887 the Sacred Congregation for the Propagation of the Faith ruled that the penal removal of any of our removable rectors could be validly accomplished only by means of a canonical process.[9]

Closer to the question at hand was the similar problem which concerned the *desservants* in France. Due to conditions in that country the Church permitted the existence of many parishes whose pastors (called *desservants*) were removable at the will of the bishop.[10] Now after the promulgation of the decree *Maxima cura* by the Sacred Congregation of the Consistory on August 20, 1910,[11] these rectors could be removed from their benefices only through the administrative removal process outlined in this decree.[12] Yet these benefices were and still are considered manual benefices.[13] Thus it is clearly evident that there were manual benefices (*amovibilia ad nutum*) whose incumbents could be removed only through an administrative process of law. This, of course, shows that the expression *amovibilia ad nutum* was understood in a much more rigid sense than its literal meaning would have implied.

[9] *Collectanea Sacrae Congregationis de Propaganda Fide* (2 vols., Romae, 1907), n. 1669. Cf. also *Fontes* (vol. VII), n. 4917. The Congregation was asked whether a canonical process was necessary for the validity of the act whereby the bishop transferred or removed a missionary rector (amovibilis) from his office of pastor. The answer was "In casibus remotionis peragendae in poenam criminis vel reatus disciplinaris, affirmative; in reliquis, negative; sed opus est ut fiant graves ob causas, et habita meritorum ratione iuxta dispositionem Concilii Plenarii Baltimoren. Tit. II, c. 5, § 32; . . ."

[10] *Thesaurus resolutionum Sacrae Congregationis Concilii* (167 vols., Romae, 1718-1908), CXXXIX (1880), 666; Bouix, *De parocho*, p. 418; Santi, *Praelectiones iuris canonici*, III, 269.

[11] *Fontes*, n. 2074.

[12] Cf. Cappello, *De administrativa remotione parochorum*, p. 119, where he comments on canon 30 of this decree.

[13] De Meester, *Iuris canonici et iuris canonico-civilis compendium*, n. 1395; Vermeersch-Creusen, *Epitome iuris canonici*, I, 390; Fanfani, *De iure parochorum*, p. 6, footnote 1.

The most practical norm to determine whether a given benefice is manual or perpetual is, quite naturally, to examine the decree whereby the benefice was erected. Under ordinary circumstances this will specifically state whether it is a perpetual (irremovable) benefice or a manual (removable) benefice. If the decre has been lost or if it does not mention this matter, the *customary* manner in which it has been conferred will evidence the nature of the benefice.[14] Finally, if custom does not demonstrate the nature of the benefice, the determining factor will be the presumption that all secular benefices are perpetual and all religious benefices manual.[15]

It is opportune at this point to pay particular attention to the consideration of parochial benefices. Under the pre-Code law one of the primary divisions among parochial benefices was that of the *paroeciae amovibiles* and the *paroeciae inamovibiles*. The former were always considered manual benefices.[16] The Code repeats this division in canon 454, § 2.[17] Therefore this present division should be interpreted just as it was before the Code.[18] Consequently the present-day removable pastors possess manual benefices. Confirming this opinion is the fact that the Code has used the two terms *parochus amovibilis* and *clericus obtinens beneficium inamovibile* in contradistinction to each other.[19] Now

[14] Schmalzgrueber, *Ius ecclesiasticum universum,* lib. III, tit. V, n. 36.

[15] Reiffenstuel, *Ius canonicum universum,* lib. III, tit. V, n. 46.

[16] Bouix, *De parocho,* pp. 208, 226, 350; Pierantonelli, *Praxis fori ecclesiastici,* p. 87; Grandclaude, *Ius canonicum iuxta ordinem decretalium* (3 vols., Parisiis, 1882), II, 406; Ballerini-Palmieri, *Opus theologicum morale,* IV, 361.

[17] "At non omnes parochi eandem obtinent stabilitatem; qui maiore gaudent, inamovibiles; qui minore, amovibiles appellari solent."

[18] Cf. canon 6, n. 2.

[19] Canon 2180: "*Parochum amovibilem* inobedientem Ordinarius statim ad normam can. 2177 coercere potest; *si vero agatur de clerico qui, beneficium inamovibile obtinens,* non paret, sed novas allegat deductiones, Ordinarius eas ad examen revocet ad normam can. 2178." Cf. also cc. 2173 and 2174.

if the Code considered the removable pastor as possessing a perpetual benefice, such a contrast would be meaningless.

Both Golden [20] and Coady [21] oppose this view. They readily admit that the religious removable pastors hold manual benefices but deny that the secular priests who are removable pastors possess manual benefices. The thought which has influenced their stand in this question is the fact that these secular removable pastors can be removed only through the administrative process outlined in the Fourth Book of the Code. From this they conclude that they are not removable *ad nutum* and hence do not hold manual benefices. Their fault lies in this that they interpret the phrase *amovibilia ad nutum* in its literal sense.

Opposed to Golden and Coady are many authors who maintain that all removable pastors possess manual benefices. Most emphatic in this stand are Vermeersch-Creusen,[22] Beste,[23] and Woywood.[24] Many others join these authors by implicitly stating this same doctrine. Thus Cocchi states that removable pastors do not possess subjective perpetuity in their benefices.[25] This is but another way of holding that they are manual benefices because those pre-Code authors who denied that manual benefices were real benefices did so because they lacked subjective perpetuity. Again Bouuaert-Simenon in commenting on canon 1576 (which rules that a collegiate tribunal of three judges must be used for the penal removal of a cleric from an irremovable bene-

[20] *Parochial benefices in the new Code*, p. 14.

[21] *The appointment of pastors*, pp. 90, 94.

[22] *Epitome iuris canonici*, III, n. 357: "Parochi amovibiles sunt ii quorum beneficium ea condicione est constitutum vel collatum, ut *ad nutum Ordinarii amoveri possint*."

[23] *Introductio in Codicem*, p. 708: "Manualia beneficia appellantur beneficia quae revocabiliter conferuntur. Quamobrem provisio paroeciarum amovibilium nunquam reservatur." Cf. p. 698 also.

[24] "The conferring of benefices"—*Homiletic and Pastoral Review*, XXIX (1929), 272-280. On p. 275 he states: "Manual benefices are those which are conferred revocably, e. g. most parishes in the United States."

[25] *Commentarium in Codicem iuris canonici*, III, 189, n. 81.

fice) remark that a collegiate tribunal would not be required to deprive a removable pastor of his benefice.[26] Obviously they could not make such a statement unless they believed that the *paroecia amovibilis* is a manual benefice and not perpetual. Wernz-Vidal likewise infer that the removable parish is but a manual benefice. Thus they state that the removable pastor does not possess a perpetual title to his benefice.[27] Then in another section of their work they maintain that the manual benefice differs from the perpetual insofar as it is not conferred *in titulum perpetuum.*[28]

In the presence of such proofs it is only logical to conclude that despite the opinion of Golden and Coady the parochial benefices held by removable pastors are manual benefices and thus are not affected by the reservations contained in the Code. Thus if the Holy See promotes a removable pastor to an episcopal see, his parochial benefice will not be reserved even though it is specifically stated in the decree of his appointment that any and all benefices he holds are reserved. The only time his removable parish would be reserved would be where the Holy See states in the decree of appointment that it is reserving any manual benefices he might possess.

b. *Benefices subject to the right of lay or mixed patronage are exempt from the reservations unless they expressly mention such benefices.*[29]

There is only one important canonical consideration involved and that centers around the fact that benefices subject to the right of ecclesiastical patronage are not exempt from the papal reservations.[30] The quality or status of the person or persons

[26] *Manuale iuris canonici*, p. 288, n. 564.

[27] *Ius canonicum*, VI, 728.

[28] *Ius canonicum*, II, 169, n. 142.

[29] Canon 1435, § 2: "At nunquam sunt reservata, nisi id expresse dicatur, beneficia manualia aut iuris patronatus laicalis vel mixti."

[30] For this division of the *ius patronatus* see canon 1449, n. 2.

who enjoy the right of patronage does not determine the type of the patronage. Thus a cleric can exercise the right of lay patronage. Rather, the determining factor is the nature of the goods or resources on which the benefice was founded. If these resources were solely eccelesiatstical, the patronage is ecclesiastical; otherwise it is mixed or lay patronage.[31]

Since it seems that none of the benefices in this country are subject to the right of patronage, this exemption is of little importance in the United States. Furthermore, in view of the fact that the Code has prohibited the establishment of the *ius patronatus* in the future,[32] there is little likelihood of any change in this regard.

c. None of the *benefices which are found in Rome* is directly subject to the reservations in the Code. Instead, these Roman benefices are conferred according to particular laws which govern this matter.[33]

As Bishop of Rome, the Pope has the ordinary right of confering all the benefices found there. Over the course of centuries, however, much of the actual conferring has passed to other clerics either by papal privilege or by custom.[34] Precisely which benefices are conferred by the Roman Pontiff is a difficult matter to determine, because, as Vermeersch-Creusen relate, numerous customs which have never been recorded in legal texts specify who is the proper authority to confer them.[35]

ARTICLE 2. THE DECRETALS "STATUTUM" AND "SI APOSTOLICA"

It seems probable that certain perpetual benefices are not reserved even though they become vacant through the death of their incumbents in Rome. This exception is based on two pre-Code

[31] Pistocchi, *De re beneficiali*, pp. 257, 258; Coronata, *op. cit.*, II, 396.

[32] Canon 1450, § 1.

[33] Canon 1435, § 3: "Quod attinet ad collationem beneficiorum quae Romae fundata sint, leges peculiares de eisdem vigentes serventur."

[34] Gonzalez, *De reservatione mensium*, gloss. XIII, n. 21.

[35] *Epitome iuris canonici*, II, 540: "Frustra conemur leges istas enumerare namque, ex parte constant usibus quorum textus legalis non exsistit."

decretals which possibly may not have been abrogated by the Code. Thus in 1274 at the II General Council of Lyons Pope Gregory X issued the decretal *Statutum*,[36] which ruled that if the Holy See did not confer a benefice within one month of its vacancy *apud Sedem*, then the one who ordinarily conferred that benefice could freely dispose of it. Later Pope Boniface VIII (1294-1303) enacted the decretal *Si Apostolica*.[37] The double effect of this law was that all parochial benefices which became vacant *apud Sedem* while the Holy See itself was vacant were not reserved, and that all parochial benefices which became vacant *apud Sedem* and were still unconferred by the Pope at the time of his death were likewise not reserved.

Before the Code the vast majority of canonists held that neither of the exceptions in these two decretals had been repealed.[38] As Linden reports, it was this opinion which was followed by the Roman Curia.[39] At the present time the canonists who have treated this question are divided as to whether the Code has abrogated these two exceptions.

Blat,[40] Prümmer,[41] Linden,[42] and Golden,[43] contend that these exceptions are still in force. They argue that canons which partially repeat the old law must be interpreted according to the old law in that part in which they agree with it.[44] Therefore since the Code repeats part of the *Licet ecclesiarum*, this part

[36] Canon 21. This was later incorporated in the *Liber Sextus* as c. 3, *De praebendis et dignitatibus*, III, 4, in VI°.

[37] C. 35, *De praebendis et dignitatibus*, III, 4, in VI°.

[38] Cf. D'Annibale, *Summula theologiae moralis*, III, 38, 39; S. D'Angelo *Parroco e parrochia*, p. 41; Sebastianelli, *Praelectiones iuris canonici*, p. 207, n. 198; Bouix, *De parocho*, p. 318.

[39] *Der Tod des Benefiziaten in Rom*, p. 250.

[40] *Commentarium textus Codicis iuris canonici*, III², 419.

[41] *Manuale iuris canonici*, p. 105.

[42] *Op. cit.*, pp. 250, 251.

[43] *Parochial benefices in the new Code*, p. 42.

[44] Cf. canon 6, n. 3.

must be interpreted according to the *Statutum* and the *Si Apostolica.*

Opposed to such a stand are Wernz-Vidal [45] and Ayrinhac.[46] The latter view seems correct to the writer. On the one hand, it seems evident that the *Si Apostolica* is opposed to the Code and thus abrogated in virtue of canon 6, n. 1. Thus the Code states that the benefices mentioned in canon 1435 are reserved to the Holy See *even though it is vacant*—". . . sunt reservata Sedi Apostolicae, quanquam vacanti . . ." [47] On the other hand, the *Statutum* appears to have been abrogated in virtue of canon 6, n. 6.[48] After all even though the *Statutum* modified the *Licet ecclesiarum,* it was a distinct disciplinary law.

It seems likely that the opinion espoused by Linden, Blat, Prümmer, and Golden is extrinsically probable. Consequently it may be safely followed in practice, especially in view of the fact that the reservation is subject to a strict interpretation. It must always be remembered, however, that these exceptions can be concerned only with one type of reserved benefice, i. e., those benefices which become vacant by death at Rome.

ARTICLE 3. BENEFICES EXEMPT THROUGH CUSTOM

Many benefices may be exempt from the reservations in the Code by a contrary custom. This doctrine that custom can abrogate a papal reservation is one which has been readily granted by canonists.[49] Under the present law, since canon 1435 does not expressly reprobate contrary customs, it is evident that many contrary customs which existed prior to the Code may still be in

[45] *Ius canonicum,* II, 252, ftn. 30.

[46] *Administrative legislation in the new Code,* p. 340.

[47] Coronata (*Institutiones iuris canonici,* II, 386, ftn. 2) favors the opinion that the *Si Apostolica* has been abrogated.

[48] " Si qua ex ceteris disciplinaribus legibus, quae usque adhuc viguerunt, nec explicite nec implicite in Codice contineatur, ea vim omnem amisisse dicenda est . . . "

[49] Sebastianelli, *Praelectiones iuris canonici,* II, 209; D'Annibale, *Summula theologiae moralis,* III, 37, ftn. 1.

force.[50] In order that a custom arising after the promulgation of the Code might derogate from any of the reservations contained in the Code, it is required that it exist for forty complete and continuous years.[51]

ARTICLE 4. THE INFLUENCE OF THE CONCORDATS

Many benefices are exempt from the reservations contained in the Code in virtue of Concordats between the Apostolic See and various civil Governments. Though such immunity may arise from either pre-Code or post-Code Concordats, the former have exercised the greater influence in this regard. In all 133 Concordats were ratified before the year 1918.[52] Most of these contained exceptions from the reservations. Now, as canon 3 rules, the exemptions contained in the Concordats which were in force at the time of the promulgation of the Code were in no way abrogated. Yet this aspect of the Concordats has been of little importance concerning the conferring of benefices under the present law because, as Cicognani remarks,[53] only a few Concordats were in force at the time of the issuance of the Code. Nevertheless the fact must be recognized that many of the Concordats, though long since abrogated, exert an indirect influence even at this late date. This influence is effected insofar as such Concordats nurtured customs and acquired rights. Thus in France at the present time the local Ordinaries confer all the benefices under their care.[54] This is a result of the abolished French Concordat of the year 1801. It is this indirect influence which represents the important exemptions from the reservations in the Code as effected by the pre-Code Concordats.

[50] Cf. canon 5.

[51] Cf. canon 27.

[52] Cf. Mercati, *Raccolta di Concordati su materie ecclesiastiche tra la S. Sede e le autorità civili* (Romae, 1919).

[53] *Canon law*, p. 470.

[54] Wernz-Vidal, *Ius canonicum*, II, 253.

Since the promulgation of the Code the Holy See has entered into agreements with more than a dozen nations.[55] These Concordats have considered for the most part the conferring of only one type of reserved benefices, i. e., the episcopal benefices.[56] It is to be noted that none of these Concordats exempts the episcopal benefice from the reservation of canon 1435. Some, however, set forth definite regulations governing the selection of the candidate. Quite generally the final selection rests with the Holy See. Before the Holy See confers the bishopric on the cleric of its choice, the usual procedure is that the name of the candidate is forwarded to the civil Government. The latter can voice a protest if the individual selected is politically objectionable to the State.

[55] Perugini (*Concordata vigentia notis historicis et iuridicis declarata* [Romae: Pontificium Institutum Utriusque Iuris, 1934]) lists most of these Concordats.

[56] There are two exceptions to this general rule. First the Roumanian Concordat rules that *curés* (pastors) are to be appointed exclusively by the local Ordinaries—*AAS*, XXI (1929), 451-456, Article XII. Secondly, a few of the Concordats determine the procedure for the conferring of dignities in cathedral and collegiate chapters, e. g., Article V of the Austrian Concordat of 1934, and Article XIV of the Bavarian Concordat of 1925—Perugini, *Concordata vigentia*, pp. 270-273; 27-28.

CHAPTER XII

Conferring of Reserved Benefices

ARTICLE 1. CONFERRING OF CONSISTORIAL BENEFICES

The conferring of a benefice ordinarily implies three distinct acts: the selection or designation of the cleric who is to receive the benefice, the granting of the title of the benefice, and the installation or the act whereby the cleric takes possession of the benefice.[1] From the juridical standpoint the second step, namely, the granting of the title, is the most important because it is through this act that the cleric receives a right to the benefice. In the conferring of all types of reserved benefices it is usually the Roman Pontiff who grants the title to the benefice acting either personally, or through his curia, or through some individual delegated with this power. To a great extent, however, the Holy See shares the exercise of the other two acts (selection of the cleric and installation) with local ecclesiastical superiors. This is significant because the first step, i. e., the selection of the cleric who is to receive the benefice, is from the practical standpoint the most important of the three acts.

In considering the conferring of consistorial benefices attention must first be focused on the process whereby the candidates are selected. This situation concerning the designation of the candidates is so varied throughout the different countries that the impossibility of presenting any plan indicative of the entire field is at once apparent. In general this much may be stated—the Holy See has granted liberal concessions to many of the parties who are interested in this selection. These concessions are outlined either in Concordats or in instructions issued by the Holy See. To give the reader some idea of the process whereby the

[1] S. d'Angelo, *Parroco e parrocchia* (3rd ed., Giarre, 1921), p. 35; Wernz-Vidal, *Ius canonicum*, II, 205.

candidates for reserved benefices are actually selected an explanation will be given of the procedure as it operates in the United States.

The following types of beneficiaries as incumbents of consistorial benefices are found in the United States: metropolitans, bishops, apostolic administrators, and abbots *nullius*. The abbots *nullius* are usually chosen through an election which must be confirmed by the Holy See.[2] Since there is no evidence of any concession by the Holy See concerning the designation of metropolitans or apostolic administrators, it appears that the Holy See exercises complete freedom in this regard. Concerning the question of episcopal appointments, however, the American hierarchy enjoys the privilege of sending a list of candidates from which the Holy See makes its choice. This represents an important concession on the part of the Holy See.

The norms whereby the American hierarchy is to propose candidates for episcopal appointments were issued by the Sacred Consistorial Congregation on July 25, 1916.[3] On alternate years the suffragan bishops are to send to their metropolitans the names of one or more priests whom they regard as likely candidates for bishoprics. The choice should be guided by the advice of their consultors and irremovable rectors. The metropolitan also proposes one or more clerics and then lists all of the names alphabetically Next all the bishops assemble and in secret session discuss the qualities of all the priests on the list. Finally they vote on the candidates and a copy of the result is forwarded to the Apostolic delegate, who will send it to the Sacred Consistorial Congregation. It is from this list that the latter will ordinarily select the new bishops for the United States.

The second act in the conferring of consistorial benefices is the granting of the title to the benefice. The title to the metropolitan or episcopal sees is granted through one of three congregations of the Roman Curia. When the see is located in a territory subject

[2] Cf. canon 320, § 1.

[3] *AAS*, VIII (1916), 400-404.

to the Sacred Congregation for the Propagation of the Faith, this congregation will grant the title.[4] When the see is situated in any other land, the title will usually be issued through the Consistorial Congregation [5] with the letter of provision proceeding from the Apostolic Chancery.[5a] The one exception in this regard is occasioned when the see is located in a State which has been conceded some power in the selection of its bishops.[6] Here the Sacred Congregation for Extraordinary Ecclesiastical Affairs is competent. Relatively the same principle seems to govern the granting of the title to Apostolic administrators. Vicars and prefects Apostolic receive their titles of possession through the Sacred Congregation for the Propagation of the Faith.[7]

The third and final step in the conferring of a consistorial benefice is the act whereby the cleric appointed takes possession of his benefice. This act is governed by a general principle, namely, that the one appointed takes valid possession of a consistorial benefice by presenting his letter of provision to the proper ecclesiastical authority, e. g., the bishop presents this letter to the cathedral chapter or diocesan consultors.[8]

ARTICLE 2. CONFERRING OF RESERVED NON-CONSISTORIAL BENEFICES

For many centuries the Holy See had allowed the local Ordinaries to recommend clerics for the reception of the reserved nonconsistorial benefices. Unfortunately no regulations of a public nature were issued to guide the bishops in this procedure. As a result the policy adopted in these applications was anything but uniform. Some bishops simply neglected to send in any recommendations. Some submitted just one name for each reserved

[4] Cf. canon 252, § 1.

[5] Cf. canon 248, § 2.

[5a] Cf. canon 260, § 1.

[6] Cf. canon 255.

[7] Cf. canon 293, § 2.

[8] Cf. canon 334, § 3. For other examples see cc. 313, § 1; 293, § 2; 353; 322, § 1.

benefice, others two names, and still others three or more names.[9] On November 11, 1930, the Apostolic Datary removed this uncertainty when it issued definite norms to regulate the manner in which the local Ordinaries should apply for the conferring of reserved benefices.[10]

In attempting to summarize this instruction it is first necessary to point out that its regulations are binding not only for the conferring of reserved benefices but also for those benefices whose conferring has devolved upon the Holy See. After this preliminary remark the local Ordinaries are warned to allow some time to pass before they have recourse to Rome. The purpose of this delay is to enable the clerics of the diocese to apply for the benefice if they so desire. Then the instruction gives the procedure for the application to be sent to the Apostolic Datary. If the benefice in question is subject to the *concursus,*[11] this is held. Then the vote of the examiners is sent to Rome together with the testimonial record of the clerics who applied. If the benefice is not subject to the *concursus,* the Ordinary sends the names of all the clerics who have applied for the benefice together with their testimonial records, i. e., records of their age, studies, life, suitability, experience. To this he adds his own report, which will be governed by the type of benefice involved. If the benefice does not entail the care of souls, the Ordinary indicates at least three clerics whom he considers more worthy for the position. If the benefice involves the care of souls, e. g., a parochial benefice, the Ordinary recommends the *one* applicant whom he deems most worthy for the office.

[9] Kinane, "Non-consistorial benefices reserved to the Holy See"—*Irish Ecclesiastical Record,* XXXVII (1931), 294, 295; *Il Monitore Ecclesiastico,* XLII (1930), 354.

[10] *AAS,* XXII (1030), 525 sq.

[11] The *concursus* is no longer required for the appointment to any parochial benefices in the United States. This was decreed by the Congregation of the Council on June 24, 1931, though not published in the *AAS*—Bouscaren, *Canon law digest,* I, 249.

The interpretation of the instruction presents very little difficulty. Indeed there is only one legal question embraced therein, namely, insofar as the Ordinaries are ordered to allow *some period of time* to elapse before they have recourse to the Apostolic Datary. The determination of the length of this delay is left to the Ordinaries. Kinane has advanced the opinion that it seems proper for the Ordinary to allow about one month to intervene between the time when the benefice becomes vacant and the time when the recourse to Rome is made.[12] This suggestion appears quite practical because it allows the local clergy ample time to apply to the Ordinary for the benefice.

It is interesting to see who installs the cleric appointed by the Apostolic Datary to a reserved benefice. According to paragraph two of canon 1443 the local Ordinary installs such a beneficiary.[13] It is the unanimous opinion of the authors, however, that this right is contingent upon the fact that the Holy See does not ordain otherwise in its decree of provision.[14] Thus, if the Apostolic Datary mentions that the possession is to be given by some cleric other than the bishop, the bishop would not be competent to install the cleric. Indeed, it seems that if he attempted this, his act would be null and void.[15]

So far emphasis has been placed on the ruling of the Code that the Apostolic Datary is the competent authority for the conferring of reserved non-consistorial benefices. It should not be inferred that the Datary is the only authority which can confer these benefices. The legates of the Holy See are partially com-

[12] Kinane, "Non-consistorial benefices reserved to the Holy See"—*Irish Ecclesiastical Record,* XXXVII (1931), 295.

[13] "Si agatur de beneficiis non consistorialibus, missio in possessionem, seu institutio corporalis, ad loci Ordinarium spectat, qui ad id alium ecclesiasticum virum delegare poterit."

[14] Wernz-Vidal, *Ius canonicum,* II, 316; Vermeersch-Creusen, *Epitome,* II, 480, n. 773; Pistocchi, *De re beneficiali,* p. 227; Cocchi, *Commentarium,* II, 252; S. d'Angelo, "De possessione beneficii"—*Apollinaris,* I (1928), 411-415, p. 413, n. 7.

[15] Sosius d'Angelo, *ibid.*, p. 414, n. 8.

petent in this regard, as is evident from their faculties.[16] Their power, however, extends only to those benefices mentioned in canon 1435, § 1, nn. 1 and 3.[17] It does not extend to other types of reserved benefices nor to those the conferring of which has devolved upon the Holy See. Furthermore, the local Ordinaries must follow the procedure just outlined if they apply to the legate for such provisions.

The final consideration of this chapter is concerned with the release of a benefice from the effects of the reservation. It has been previously mentioned that most reserved benefices return to the power of the local Ordinaries as soon as the Holy See has conferred them. There has been some discussion regarding the precise moment at which one may say that the benefice has been conferred. The discussion centers around the canonical possession of the benefice, namely, whether the canonical possession is to be regarded as an essential part of the conferring. This problem may be illustrated by the following example. The Apostolic Datary sends out a decree conferring a reserved benefice on a certain cleric. Let it be supposed that the cleric died before he took possession of the benefice. Would that benefice still be reserved, or would it have returned to the power of the local Ordinary?

Many of the pre-Code canonists held that such a benefice could be freely conferred by the local Ordinary, i. e., that it was no longer reserved. They reasoned that in the strict meaning of the terms there is a difference between the conferring of a benefice and the canonical possession of the same. Therefore, since the

[16] Bouscaren, *Canon law digest,* I, 176; *Periodica,* XII (1923), 72; *Il Monitore Ecclesiastico,* XXXII (1920), 138, n. 4.

[17] Canon 1435, § 1, n. 1: "Omnia beneficia, etiam curata, quae vacaverint per obitum, promotionem, renuntiationem, vel translationem S. R. E. Cardinalium, Legatorum Romani Pontificis, officialium maiorum Sacrarum Congregationum, Tribunalium et Officiorum Romanae Curiae et Familiarum, etiam honoris tantum, Summi Pontificis tempore vacationis beneficii."

n. 3: "Quae invalide ob simoniae vitium collata fuerint."

reservation must be interpreted strictly, a benefice can cease to be reserved even though the one appointed does not obtain possession of that benefice.[18] It seems probable, however, that this opinion is no longer tenable. The Code itself is silent on this point. Therefore the style and practice of the Roman Curia can supply the proper norm to settle this point.[19] Now, as d'Angelo notes,[20] the Apostolic Datary has clearly evidenced its intention of considering a benefice reserved until the conferring has been completed by the canonical possession of the benefice. Certainly this seems the safer opinion to follow in practice.

[18] Lotterius, *De re beneficiaria,* II, q. XXVI, n. 39: "Eatenus durat reservatio, quatenus provisio consumitur. Intelligitur autem consumpta, sive provisus possessionem apprehenderit, sive non, cum possessio fit quid penitus separatum a provisione, per quam consumitur vacatio, ut respondit Rota decis. 512 . . ."; Garcia, *De beneficiis ecclesiasticis,* pars IV, cap. II, n. 2: "Unde per collationem secuta acceptatione sine possessione expirat reservatio . . ."; Gonzalez, *De reservatione mensium,* gloss. XV, sectio II, n. 37.

[19] Cf. canon 20.

[20] "De reservatione beneficii"—*Apollinaris,* II (1929), 511-515, p. 513 sub litteris "e" et "f".

CHAPTER XIII

Ecclesiastical Benefices and the Reservations in the United States

ARTICLE 1. ECCLESIASTICAL BENEFICES IN THE UNITED STATES

Motivated by a private reply of the Pontifical Commission for the Authentic Interpretation of the Code on September 26, 1921,[1] the American authors have adopted a rather uniform stand on the existence of benefices in the United States.[2] Following the observation of the late Cardinal Bonzano (then the Apostolic Delegate) on this reply of the Code Commission,[3] they maintain that every parish in this country is a real benefice provided it possesses the following three characteristics: (1) a resident pastor; (2) endowment according to canons 1410 and 1415, § 3; and (3) boundaries. In applying this principle to our parishes they conclude, and probably too cautiously, that *most* American parishes are benefices.

It seems to the writer that the conditions in this country postulate a more extensive conclusion, namely, that almost all the parishes in the United States constitute real benefices. The authors have refrained from such a broad conclusion primarily because they doubt that our national parishes are benefices.[4] The reason for this stand is the allegation that national parishes do not have strict boundaries. As a matter of fact, however, a glance at almost any of the diocesan directories reveals that most of these parishes do have definite boundaries. In other words, even

[1] Bouscaren, *Canon law digest*, I, 149.

[2] Golden, *Parochial benefices in the new Code*, pp. 97-107; Coady, *The appointment of pastors*, pp. 65-77; Augustine, *Rights and duties of Ordinaries*, pp. 359, 360; Connolly, *The canonical erection of parishes*, pp. 90, 91.

[3] Bouscaren, *ibid.*

[4] Augustine, *A commentary on canon law*, VI, 495; Ayrinhac, *Constitution of the Church*, p. 25.

though they are personal parishes, at the same time they are also territorial.[5] Consequently they should be regarded as real parishes and hence as benefices. Thus it seems likely that almost every parish in the United States is a real benefice. It should be noted, however, that most of our parishes have removable pastors and therefore are only manual benefices.

Little consideration has been given by American authors to the possible existence of minor benefices in the United States other than parochial benefices. It is at once obvious that there are many ecclesiastical offices in this country which would supply a suitable basis for ecclesiastical benefices. A few examples of offices which could be erected into benefices would be parochial assistantships, chaplaincies, and rectorships of seminaries. The important question is, of course, whether any ecclesiastical superiors have erected any of these offices as benefices. The complete lack of any notice of such action prompts a negative reply. Thus it seems likely that the only minor ecclesiastical benefices in the United States are our parishes.

ARTICLE 2. THE RESERVATIONS IN THE UNITED STATES

Canon 1435, which contains all the present reservations, represents a part of the common law of the Church. Since the Church in the United States is subject to the common law embraced in the Code, the first impression naturally is that the reservations are in force in this country. Both Augustine[6] and Woywood[7] are inclined to believe, however, that the only reserved benefices in the United States are the consistorial benefices. Thus they maintain that the parochial benefices in this country are not subject to the reservations in the Code though they make no effort

[5] Cappello, *Summa iuris canonici*, II, p. 11, n. 488: "Plerumque paroecia *personalis* est quoque *territorialis*, quatenus complectitur fideles qui commorantur in hoc pago vel civitate, et non extra."

[6] *The canonical and civil status of Catholic parishes in the United States* (St. Louis: Herder Book Co., 1926), pp. 150, 210.

[7] "Conferring of benefices"—*Homiletic and Pastoral Review*, XXIX (1929), 273, 275.

to prove their assertion. That opinion must be regarded as erroneous. After all, if the benefices in the United States were exempt from the reservations, such exemption would necessarily arise from a concordat, from a papal indult, from acquired rights, or from lawful custom. Actually no such source of exemption exists and hence our parochial benefices are subject to the reservations in canon 1435.

By far the greater percentage of parishes in the United States are *paroeciae amovibiles* and therefore are manual benefices. That is an important fact to stress for it implies that under ordinary circumstances these benefices are not reserved. Thus, if a removable pastor dies in Rome, the local Ordinary can freely confer that parish. The only case wherein *paroeciae amovibiles* will be reserved is had when the Roman Pontiff expressly mentions that he is reserving manual benefices. The *paroeciae inamovibiles* in this country, however, are perpetual benefices and are fully subject to the reservations in the Code.

In conclusion a few words will be devoted to the legal factor of custom. It will be considered insofar as it could acquire the force to abrogate the reservations in the United States. Since this country did not become subject to the common law of the Church (hence neither to the reservations) until the issuance of the Constitution, *Sapienti consilio* in the year 1908,[8] there can be no question of any contrary custom prior to that date. Between the years 1908 and 1918 (the advent of the Code), however, it seems likely that there were minor benefices (the *paroeciae inamovibiles*) in the United States subject to the papal reservations of that period. Consequently, it is possible that there was in existence a custom contrary to the reservations. Even if such a custom did exist, however, it was certainly abolished with the advent of the Code.[9] Thus the year 1918 is the earliest possible

[8] *Fontes*, n. 682.

[9] Cf. canon 5: "... aliae (consuetudines), quae quidem centennariae sint et immemorabiles, tolerari poterunt si Ordinarii pro locorum ac personarum adiunctis existimet eas prudenter submoveri non posse; *ceterae suppressae habeantur*, nisi expresse Codex aliud caveat."

date for the beginning of a usage contrary to the reservations here in the United States. This means that if the bishops of a certain section of this country have been of the opinion that Rome did not wish the reservations to be in force in the United States and have conferred all the benefices themselves, such a contrary usage at the present time could be of only twenty-four years' duration. Since forty years is the minimum temporal requirement in order that usage may become a custom which can effectively derogate from one of the laws in the Code,[10] it is apparent that nowhere in the United States has custom derogated the reservations in canon 1435. Thus it is elear that the reservations do bind in the United States.

[10] Cf. canon 27: "...sed neque iuri ecclesiastico praeiudicium affert (consuetudo), nisi fuerit rationabilis et legitime per annos quadraginta continuos et completos praescripta."

CONCLUSIONS

THE more important conclusions reached in this study of reserved benefices may be summarized as follows:

(1) The early stages of the system of reserved benefices must be regarded as an offensive weapon against lay domination of the ecclesiastical benefice—either as a necessary corollary or as an essential complement of the Gregorian Reform. The attacks which have branded the start of this system as a manifestation of papal greed are devoid of credibility.

(2) The first general reservation was issued in the *Licet ecclesiarum* in the year 1265. The earlier "*antiqua consueudo*" mentioned in this decretal was nothing more than a custom whereby the previous Popes had conferred certain benefices by the *ius concursus* and not by the *ius reservationis.*

(3) Most of the reserved benefices cease to be reserved as soon as the Holy See confers them. The two exceptions in this regard are consistorial benefices and dignities in cathedral and collegiate chapters.

(4) Regarding the reservation of the benefices of members of the papal household one must hold that such benefices are reserved only when the cleric in question was actually a member of the papal household at the very moment the benefice became vacant.

(5) If circumstances should compel the Roman Pontiff to dwell in a city other than Rome, the benefice of a cleric who died in such a city would not be reserved in virtue of canon 1435, § 1, n. 2 (i. e., "*per obitum in ipsa Urbe*").

(6) When a cleric dies in Rome, the consequent reservation of his benefice in no way depends on the reason which motivated his presence in that City. Thus it will be reserved even if his death occurred while he was there on a pleasure trip.

(7) The parishes held by removable pastors are manual benefices. Therefore they are never reserved in law unless a specific reservation expressly mentions them.

(8) While the writer does not subscribe to the opinion of those who maintain that when a benefice is reserved because of the death of the incumbent in Rome, it ceases to be reserved if the Pope does not confer it within one month, it is safe to follow this opinion in practice. Likewise one can follow the opinion which states that parochial benefices are not reserved if their incumbents die in Rome while the Holy See is vacant. Again one may safely hold that a parochial benefice vacant by the death of the incumbent in Rome ceases to be reserved if it is still unconferred at the death of the Pope.

(9) The reservations listed in canon 1435 are in effect in the United States.

BIBLIOGRAPHY

Sources

Bullarium diplomatum et privilegiorum sanctorum Romanorum Pontificum Taurinensis editio, 25 vols., Augustae Taurinorum, 1857-1872.

Canones et decreta sacrosancti oecumenici Concilii Tridentini, Romae: ex typographia polyglotta S. C. de Propaganda Fide, 1882.

Codex iuris canonici Pii X Pontificis maximi iussu digestus Benedicti XV auctoritate promulgatus, Romae, 1917.

Codicis iuris canonici fontes, cura Emi Petri Card. Gasparri editi, 9 vols., Romae (postea civitate Vaticana): typis polyglottis Vaticanis, 1923-1939 (vols. VII, VIII, et IX ed. cura et studio Emi. Iustiniani Card. Serédi).

Collectanea S. Congregationis de Propaganda Fide, 2 vols., Romae, 1907.

Corpus iuris canonici, editio Lipsiensis, Aemilius Ludovicus Richter—Aemilius Friedberg, 2 vols., Lipsiae, 1879-1881. Editio anastatice repetita, 1928.

Evans, William, *A collection of statutes*, 7 vols., London, 1817.

Jaffe, *Regesta Pontificum ab condita Ecclesia ad annum post Christum natum MCXCVIII*, 2nd ed., cura Wattenbach, Löwenfeld, Kaltenbrunner, Ewald, 2 vols. in 1, Lipsiae, 1885-1888.

Liber Sextus decretalium una cum Clementinis et Extravagantibus earumque glossis restitutis, Romae, 1582.

Mansi, J. D., *Conciliorum sacrorum nova et amplissima collectio*, 53 vols. in 59, Paris, Arnhem, Leipzig, 1901-1927.

Migne, J. P., *Patrologiae cursus completus*—series Latina, 221 vols., Parisiis, 1844-1864.

Mollat, G., *Jean XXII (1316-1334), Lettres communes*, 14 vols., Paris: Boccard, 1904-1935.

Monumenta Germaniae historica, Epistolae selectae, tom. II, *Das Register Gregors VII*, 2 fasc., ed. Erich Caspar, Berolini: apud Weidmannos, 1920-1925.

Monumenta Germaniae historica, Legum I, ed. Pertz, Leipzig, 1925.

Monumenta Germaniae historica, Legum Sectio II, Capitularia regum Francorum, tom. I, ed. A. Boretius, Hannoverae, 1883.

Monumenta Germaniae historica, Legum Sectio III, Concilia aevi Merovingici, ed. F. Maasen, Hannoveriae, 1893.

Monumenta Germaniae historica, Legum Sectio III, Concilia, tom. II, pars I, ed. A. Werminghoff, Berlin, 1904.

Monumenta Germaniae historica, Legum Sectio IV, Constitutiones et acta publica regum, tom. I, ed. L. Weiland, Berlin, 1892.

Ottenthal, E., *Regulae cancellariae apostolicae, die Päpstlichen Kanzleiregeln von Johannes XXII bis Nicholaus V*, Innsbruck, 1888.

Potthast, Augustus, *Regesta Pontificum Romanorum*, Berolini, 1874-1875.

Regulae cancellariae apostolicae S.D.N. Gregorii Papae XIV, Romae, 1590.

Regulae cancellariae apostolicae S.D.N. Alexandri Papae VII, Romae, 1655.

Regulae cancellariae apostolicae S.N.N. Alexandri Papae VIII, Romae, 1689.

Regulae cancellariae apostolicae S.D.N. Benedicti Papae XIII, Romae, 1724.

Registres de Clement IV, published by E. Jordan, Paris, 1893-1912.

Registres d'Urbain IV, ed. J. Guiraud, Paris, 1901-1925.

Sacrae Romanae Rotae decisiones nuperrimae, 10 vols., pro annis 1884-1706, Romae, n. d.

Sacrae Romanae Rotae decisiones recentiores, ed. Farinacius, Rubeus, et Compagnus, 25 vols., Venetiis, 1697.

Thesaurus resolutionum Sacrae Congregationis Concilii, 167 vols., Romae, 1718-1908.

AUTHORS

Albers, P., *Enchiridion historiae ecclesiasticae universae*, 3rd ed., 3 vols., Neomagi, 1910.

Ayrinhac, H. A., *Administrative legislation in the new Code of canon law*, New York; Longmans, Green & Co., 1930.

——, *Constitution of the Church in the new Code of canon law*, New York: Longmans, Green & Co., 1930.

(Bachofen), Charles Augustine, *The canonical and civil status of Catholic parishes in the United States*, St. Louis: Herder Co., 1926.

——, *A commentary on the new Code of canon law*, 8 vols., St. Louis: Herder Co., vol. VI, 1921.

Ballerini-Palmieri, *Opus theologicum morale*, 7 vols., Prati, 1889-1893.

Barbosa, Augustinus, *De officio et potestate episcopi*, 3 vols. in 1, Lugduni, 1628.

Barraclough, Geoffrey, *Papal provisions*, Oxford: Basil Blackwell, 1935.

Beste, Udalricus, *Introductio in Codicem*, Collegeville, Minn.: St. John's Abbey Press, 1938.

Blat, Albertus, *Commentarium textus Codicis iuris canonici*, 5 vols. in 6, Vol. III^2, *De rebus*, Romae: Collegio Angelico, 1923.

Bouix, D., *Tractatus de parocho*, Parisiis, 1855.

Bouscaren, T., *Canon law digest*, 2 vols. and supplement, Milwaukee: Bruce Publishing Co., 1934-1941.

Cambridge medieval history, the, planned by J. Bury and edited by Gwatkin and Whitney, 8 vols., New York: Macmillan & Co., 1911-1936.

Cavagnis, Felix, *Institutiones iuris publici ecclesiastici*, 4th ed., 3 vols., Romae, 1906.

Cavanagh, A., *Pope Gregory and the theocratic state*, Washington, D. C., 1934.

Cappello, Felix, *De administrativa amotione parochorum seu commentarium in decretum "Maxima cura"*, Romae, 1911.

——, *De curia romana iuxta reformationem a Pio X sapientissime inductam*, 2 vols., Romae, 1911-1912.

——, *Summa iuris canonici*, 3 vols., vol. II, Romae: Universitas Gregoriana, 1930.

——, *Summa iuris publici ecclesiastici*, 2nd ed., Romae: Universitas Gregoriana, 1928.

Cavigioli, G. *Manuale de diritto canonico*, Torino: Societa editrice internazionale, 1934.

Chelodi-Bertagnolli, *Ius de personis iuxta Codicem iuris canonici*, 2nd ed., Tridenti: Libr. edit. Tridentum, 1927.

Chokier, Ioannes, *Commentaria in regulas cancellariae apostolicae*, Coloniae Agrippinae, 1674.

Cicognani, Amleto, *Canon law*, authorized English version by J. O'Hara and F. Brennan, Philadelphia; Dolphin Press, 1934.

Claeys-Bouuaert, F. et Simenon, G., *Manuale iuris canonici*, 2nd ed., Gandae et Leodii: Seminarium Gandavense et Leodiense, 1926.

Coady, John, *The appointment of pastors*, Catholic University of America, Canon Law Studies, n. 52, Washington, D. C.: The Catholic University of America, 1929.

Cocchi, Guidus, *Commentarium in Codicem iuris canonici ad usum scholarum*, 8 vols., vol. III, *De rebus*, Romae: Marietti, 1924.

Connolly, Nicholas, *The canonical erection of parishes*, Catholic University of America Canon Law Studies, n. 114, Washington, D. C.: Catholic University Press, 1938,

Coronata, Matthaeus Conte a, *Institutiones iuris canonici*, 5 vols., Taurini: Marietti, 1928-1936.

d'Angelo, Sosius, *Parroco e parrocchia*, 3rd ed., Giarre, 1921.

D'Annibale, Josephus, *Summula theologiae moralis*, 3rd ed., 3 vols., Romae, 1892.

De Meester, Alphonsus, *Iuris canonici et iuris canonico-civilis compendium*, nova ed., 3 vols. in 4, Brugis: Desclée & Co., 1921-1928.

Fanfani, Ludovicus, *De iure parochorum*, ed. altera, Taurini: Marietti, 1936.

Fischer, G., *The medieval empire*, 2 vols., London, 1898.

Funk, F. X., *Manual of Church history*, 2 vols., translated from the German by Perciballi and edited by Kent, London: Burns, Oates & Washbourne, Ltd., 1931.

Garcia, Nicolaus, *Tractatus de beneficiis*, Coloniae Allobrogum, 1636.

Gennari, Casimir, *Quistioni canoniche*, 2nd ed., Romae, 1908.

Golden, H. F., *Parochial benefices in the new Code*, Catholic University of America, Canon Law Studies, n. 10, Washington, D. C.: Catholic University Press, 1921.

Gonzalez, Hieronymus, *Glossema seu commentatio ad regulam octavam cancellariae, de reservatione mensium*, Romae, 1604.

Grandclaude, Eugenius, *Ius canonicum iuxta ordinem decretalium*, 3 vols., Parisiis, 1882-1883.

Grosseteste, Robertus, *Epistolae*, ed. by H. R. Luard, Rolls series, London, 1861.

Hinschius, Paul, *System des katholischen Kirchenrechts*, 4 vols., Berlin, 1869-1888.

Hostiensis, Cardinalis (Henricus de Segusio), *Commentaria in Quinque Decretalium Libros*, 5 vols., Venetiis, 1581.

Imbart de la Tour, Pierre, *De ecclesiis rusticanis aetate carolingica*, Burdegale, 1890.

——, *Les elections episcopales dans l'Eglise de France du IXe au XIIe siècle*, Paris, 1890.

Ioannes de Selua, *Tractatus de beneficio*, n. p., 1513.

Leurenius, Petrus, *Forum beneficiale*, 2 parts in 1, Venetiis, 1742.

Linden, Peter, *Der Tod des Benefiziaten in Rom*, Bonn: Ludwig Roehrscheid, 1938.

Lotterius, Melchoir, *De re beneficiaria*, nova ed., 3 vols. in 1, Patavii, 1700.

Lux, Carolus, *Constitutionum apostolicarum de generali beneficiorum reservatione ab anno 1266 usque ad annum 1378*, Wratislaviae, 1904.

Maroto, Philip, *Institutiones iuris canonici ad normam novi Codicis*, 3rd ed., 2 vols., Romae: Apud Commentarium pro Religiosis, 1921.

Matthaeus Parisiensis, *Chronica maiora*, ed. by H. R. Luard, Rolls series, 7 vols., London, 1872-1883.

Meier, Carl, *Penal administrative procedure against negligent pastors*, Catholic University of America, Canon Law Studies, n. 140, Washington, D. C.: Catholic University Press, 1941.

Mercati, *Raccolta di concordati su materie ecclesiastiche tra la S. Sede e le autorita civili*, Romae, 1919.

Mollat, G., *La collation des benefices ecclésiastiques sous les Papes d'Avignon*, Paris: Fontemoing & Cie., 1921.

Nainfa, *Costume of prelates of the Catholic Church*, 2nd ed., Baltimore, 1926.

Ojetti, B., *Commentarium in Codicem iuris canonici*, 4 vols., Romae: Universitas Gregoriana, 1927-1931.

Ottaviani, A., *Institutiones iuris publici ecclesiastici*, 2nd ed., 2 vols., Typis Polyglottis Vaticanis, 1935-1936.

Parsons, Anscar, *Canonical elections*, The Catholic University of America, Canon Law Studies, n. 118, Washington, D. C.: Catholic University Press, 1940.

Perugini, Angelus, *Concordata vigentia notis historicis et iuridicis declarata*, Romae: Pontificum Institutum Utriusque Iuris, 1934.

Phillips, G., *Kirchenrecht*, 8 vols., Regensburg, 1845-1889, vol. VIII by F. Vering.

Pierantonelli, Pacificus, *Praxis fori ecclesiastici*, Romae, 1883.

Pistocchi, Marius, *De re beneficiali*, Taurini: Marietti, 1928.

Political history of England, The, ed. by W. Hunt and R. Poole, 12 vols., London, 1906-1907, vol. III by T. F. Tout.

Prümmer, Dominicus, M., *Manuale iuris canonici*, 6th ed., Friburgi Brisgoviae: Herder Co., 1933.

Quesada y Molina, Rodericus de, *Notae seu indices breves ad regulas cancellariae apostolicae S.D.N. Gregorii XV*, Romae, 1622.

Reiffenstuel, Anacletus, *Ius canonicum universum*, 5 vols. in 7, Parisiis, 1864-1870.

Riganti, Ioannes B., *Commentaria in regulas, constitutiones, et ordinationes cancellariae apostolicae*, 4 vols. in 2, Coloniae Allobrogum, 1751.

Rossi, Joseph, *De paroecia iuxta Codicem iuris canonici*, Romae: Pustet, 1923.

Ryder, Raymond, *Simony*, Catholic University of America Canon Law Studies, n. 65, Washington, D. C.: Catholic University Press, 1931.

Sägmuller, I., *Lehrbuch des katholischen Kirchenrechts*, 4th ed., vol. I, 4 fascicles, Freiburgi Br., 1925-1934.

Sanguinetti, S., *Institutiones iuris ecclesiastici privati*, Romae, 1884.

Santi, Franciscus-Leitner, Martinus, *Praelectiones iuris canonici*, 5 vols. in 3, Ratisbonae, 1898-1899.

Scavini, Petrus, *Theologia moralis universa ad mentem S. Alphonsi M. de Ligorio*, 11th ed., 4 vols., Mediolani, 1869.

Scherer, Rudolph Ritter von, *Handbuch des Kirchenrechtes*, 2 vols., Graz-Leipzig, 1886-1898.

Schmalzgrueber, Franciscus, *Ius ecclesiasticum universum*, 5 vols. in 12, Romae, 1843-1845.

Sebastianelli, Guilelmus, *Praelectiones iuris canonici*, 2nd ed., 3 vols., Romae, 1905.

Simeone, Gennaro, *Lezioni di diritto canonico*, 2 vols., vol. II, 3rd ed., 1905.

Sipos, Stephanus, *Enchiridion iuris canonici*, Pecs (Hungary), 1926.

Smith, A. L., *Church and state in the Middle Ages*, Oxford, 1913.

Soglia, Ioannes, *Institutiones iuris ecclesiastici publici et privati*, 2 vols., Neapoli, 1864.

Thomassinus, Ludovicus, *Vetus et nova ecclesiae disciplina circa beneficia et beneficiarios*, 3 vols., Lucae, 1728.

Van Hove, A., *Prolegomena ad Codicem iuris canonici*, Commentarium Lovaniense, Vol. I, tom. I, Mechliniae, et Romae: Dessain, 1928.

Vermeersch, Arturus et Creusen, Josephus, *Epitome iuris canonici*, 3 vols., Mechliniae: H. Dessain, Vol. I, 5th ed., 1934; Vol. II, 5th ed., 1936; Vol. III, 6th ed., 1937.

Weier, Joseph, *Der kanonische Weiheititel*, Würzburg: Richard Mayr, 1936.

Wernz, Franciscus, *Ius decretalium*, 6 vols., Romae et Prati, 1898-1905.

Wernz, F. et Vidal, P., *Ius canonicum*, 7 tom. in 8, Romae: Apud Aedes Universitatis Gregorianae, 1923-1938.

Principal Articles

Bersani, Francesco, " Le innovazioni del codice circa il conferimento dei benefici "—*Il Monitore Ecclesiastico*, XXX (1918), 341-348.

d'Angelo, Sosius, " De possessione beneficii "—*Apollinaris*, I (1928), 411-415.

——, " De reservatione beneficii "—*Apollinaris*, II (1929), 511-515.

——, " De collatione beneficii et dignitatum "—*Apollinaris*, III (1930),

322-325.

Göller, Emil, " Die Kommentatoren der päpstlichen Kanzleiregeln vom Ende des 17 Jahrhunderts "—*AKKR*, LXXXV (1905), 441-460.

——, " Zur Geschichte des zweiten Lyoner Konzils und des *Liber Sextus* " —*Römische Quartalschrift*, XX (1906), 81-87.

Hilling, N., " Was bedeutet der Zusatz ' tempore vacationis beneficii ' in can. 1435, § 1, n. 1 CJC "—*AKKR*, CIV (1924), 282-287.

Kinane, J., " Non-consistorial benefices reserved to the Holy See "—*Irish Ecclesiastical Record*, XXXVII (1931), 294-295.

Maroto, Philippus, " Normae servandae ab Ordinariis "—*Apollinaris*, IV (1931), 51-55.

Oestrich, Thomas, " The Hildebrandine reform and its latest historian "—*Catholic Historical Review*, XVII (1931-1932), 256-261.

Schaefer, H. K., " Zur Kritik mittelalterlicher kirchlicher Zustände "—*Römische Quartalschrift*, XX (1906), 123-141.

Sipos, Stephanus, " Quid significent verba ' temporis vacationis ' in can. 1435, par. 1, n. 1 CJC ? "—*AKKR*, CVI (1926), 575-576.

Stutz, U., " The proprietary churches as an element of medieval Germanic law "—*Medieval German essays*, II, translated by Barraclough, pp. 35-70, Oxford: Blackwell, 1938.

PERIODICALS

Apollinaris, Commentarium Iuridico-Canonicum, Romae, 1928—

Archiv für katholisches Kirchenrecht, Innsbruck, 1857-1861; Mainz, 1862—

Catholic Historical Review, Washington, 1920—

English Historical Review, London, 1886—

Monitore Ecclesiastico, Il, Romae, 1876—

Irish Ecclesiastical Record, Dublin, 1864—

Periodica de Re Canonica et Morali utili Praesertim Religiosis et Missionariis, Bruges, 1905—

Römische Quartalschrift, Romae, 1893—

ABBREVIATIONS

AAS—*Acta Apostolicae Sedis.*

AKKR—*Archiv für katholisches Kirchenrecht.*

Fontes—*Codicis iuris canonici fontes cura . . . Gasparri editi.*

Ftn.—footnote.

MGH—*Monumenta Germaniae historica.*

MPG—Migne, *Patrologia Graeca.*

MPL—Migne, *Patrologia Latina.*

Mansi—*Sacrorum conciliorum nova et amplissima collectio.*

BIOGRAPHICAL NOTE

John Joseph Haydt was born October 19, 1913, in Philadelphia, Pennsylvania. There he attended Saint Columba's Parochial School, Roman Catholic High School, and Northeast Catholic High School. In the Fall of 1931 he entered the Seminary of Saint Charles Borromeo receiving the Bachelor of Arts degree in June, 1935. He was ordained to the sacred priesthood on June 3, 1939, by His Eminence, Dennis Cardinal Dougherty, Archbishop of Philadelphia. In the Fall of the same year he was sent to the Catholic University of America, from which he received the Baccalaureate in Canon Law in June, 1940, and the Licentiate in Canon Law in June, 1941.

ANALYTICAL INDEX

CANON LAW STUDIES

1. Freriks, Rev. Celestine A., C.PP.S., J.C.D., Religious Congregations in Their External Relations, 121 pp., 1916.
2. Galliher, Rev. Daniel M., O.P., J.C.D., Canonical Elections, 117 pp., 1917.
3. Borkowski, Rev. Aurelius L., O.F.M., J.C.D., De Confraternitatibus Ecclesiasticis, 136 pp., 1918.
4. Castillo, Rev. Cayo, J.C.D., Disertación Historico-Canonica sobre la Potestad del Cabildo en Sede Vacante o Impedida del Vicario Capitular, 99 pp., 1919 (1918).
5. Kubelbeck, Rev. William J., S.T.B., J.C.D., The Sacred Penitentiaria and its Relations to Faculties of Ordinaries and Priests, 129 pp., 1918.
6. Petrovits, Rev. Joseph, J.C., S.T.D., J.C.D., The New Church Law On Matrimony, X-461 pp., 1919.
7. Hickey, Rev. John J., S.T.B., J.C.D., Irregularities and Simple Impediments in the Uew Code of Canon Law, 100 pp., 1920.
8. Klekotka, Rev. Peter J., S.T.B., J.C.D., Diocesan Consultors, 179 pp., 1920.
9. Wanenmacher, Rev. Francis, J.C.D., The Evidence in Ecclesiastical Procedure Affecting the Marriage Bond, 1920 (Printed 1935).
10. Golden, Rev. Henry Francis, J.C.D., Parochial Benefices in the New Code, IV-119 pp., 1921 (Printed 1925).
11. Koudelka, Rev. Charles J., J.C.D., Pastors, Their Rights and Duties According to the New Code of Canon Law, 211 pp., 1921.
12. Melo, Rev. Antonius, O.F.M., J.C.D., De Exemptione Regularium, X-188 pp., 1921.
13. Schaaf, Rev. Valentine Theodore, O.F.M., S.T.B., J.C.D., The Cloister, X-180 pp., 1921.
14. Burke, Rev. Thomas Joseph, S.T.D., J.C.D., Competence in Ecclesiastical Tribunals, IV-117 pp., 1922.
15. Leech, Rev. George Leo, J.C.D., A Comparative Study of the Constitution, "Apostolicae Sedis" and the "Codex Juris Canonici," 179 pp., 1922.
16. Motry, Rev. Hubert Louis, S.T.D., J.C.D., Diocesan Faculties According to the Code of Canon Law, II-167 pp., 1922.
17. Murphy, Rev. George Lawrence, J.C.D., Delinquencies and Penalties in the Administration and Reception of the Sacraments, IV-121 pp., 1923.
18. O'Reilly, Rev. John Anthony, S.T.B., J.C.D., Ecclesiastical Sepulture in the New Code of Canon Law, II-129 pp., 1923.
19. Michalicka, Rev. Wenceslas Cyrill, O.S.B., J.C.D., Judicial Procedure in Dismissal of Clerical Exempt Religious, 107 pp., 1923.

20. Dargin, Rev. Edward Vincent, S.T.B., J.C.D., Reserved Cases According to the Code of Canon Law, IV-103, pp. 1924.
21. Godfrey, Rev. John A., S.T.B., J.C.D., The Right of Patronage According to the Code of Canon Law, 153 pp., 1924.
22. Hagedorn, Rev. Francis Edward, J.C.D., General Legislation on Indulgences, II-154 pp., 1924.
23. King, Rev. James Ignatius, J.C.D., The Administration of the Sacraments to Dying Non-Catholics, V-141 pp., 1924.
24. Winslow, Rev. Francis Joseph, O.F.M., J.C.D., Vicars and Prefects Apostolic, IV-149 pp., 1924.
25. Correa, Rev. Jose Servelion, S.T.L., J.C.D., La Potestad Legislativa de la Iglesia Catolica, IV-127 pp., 1925.
26. Dugan, Rev. Henry Francis, A.M., J.C.D., The Judiciary Department of the Diocesan Curia, 87 pp., 1925.
27. Keller, Rev. Charles Frederick, S.T.B., J.C.D., Mass Stipends, 167 pp., 1925.
28. Paschang, Rev. John Linus, J.C.D., The Sacramentals According to the Code of Canon Law, 129 pp., 1925.
29. Piontek, Rev. Cyrillus, O.F.M., S.T.B., J.C.D., De Indulto Exclaustrationis necnon Saecularizationis, XIII-289 pp., 1925.
30. Kearney, Rev. Richard Joseph, S.T.B., J.C.D., Sponsors at Baptism According to the Code of Canon Law, IV-127 pp., 1925.
31. Bartlett, Rev. Chester Joseph, A.M., LL.B., J.C.D., The Tenure of Parochial Property in the United States of America, V-108 pp., 1926.
32. Kilker, Rev. Adrian Jerome, J.C.D., Extreme Unction, V-425 pp., 1926.
33. McCormick, Rev. Robert Emmett, J.C.D., Confessors of Religious, VIII-266 pp., 1926.
34. Miller, Rev. Newton Thomas, J.C.D., Founded Masses According to the Code of Canon Law, VII-93 pp., 1926.
35. Roelker, Rev. Edward G., S.T.D., J.C.D., Principles of Privilege According to the Code of Canon Law, XI-166 pp., 1926.
36. Bakalarczyk, Rev. Richardus, M.I.C., J.U.D., De Novitiatu, VIII-208 pp., 1927.
37. Pizzuti, Rev. Lawrence, O.F.M., J.U.L., De Parochis Religiosis, 1927 (Not printed).
38. Bliley, Rev. Nicholas Martin, O.S.B., J.C.D., Altars According to the Code of Canon Law, XIX-132 pp., 1927.
39. Brown, Mr. Brendan Francis, A.B., LL.M., J.U.D., The Canonical Juristic Personality with Special Reference to Its Status in the United States of America, V-212 pp., 1927.
40. Cavanaugh, Rev. William Thomas, C.P., J.U.D., The Reservation of the Blessed Sacrament, VIII-101 pp., 1927.
41. Doheny, Rev. William J., C.S.C., A.B., J.U.D., Church Property: Modes of Acquisition, X-118 pp., 1927.
42. Feldhaus, Rev. Aloysius H., C.PP.S., J.C.D., Oratories, IX-141 pp., 1927.

43. Kelly, Rev. James Patrick, A.B., J.C.D., The Jurisdiction of the Simple Confessor, X-208 pp., 1927.
44. Neuberger, Rev. Nicholas J., J.C.D., Canon 6 or the Relation of the Codex Juris Canonici to the Preceding Legislation, V-95 pp., 1927.
45. O'Keefe, Rev. Gerald Michael, J.C.D., Matrimonial Dispensations, Powers of Bishops, Priests and Confessors, VIII-232 pp., 1927.
46. Quigley, Rev. Joseph, A.B., A.M., J.C.D., Condemned Societies, 139 pp., 1927.
47. Zaplotnik, Rev. Johannes Leo, J.C.D., De Vicariis Foraneis, X-142 pp., 1927.
48. Duskie, Rev. John Aloysius, A.B., J.C.D., The Canonical Status of the Orientals in the United States, VIII, 196 pp., 1928.
49. Hyland, Rev. Francis Edward, J.C.D., Excommunication, Its Nature, Historical Development and Effects, VIII-181 pp., 1928.
50. Reinmann, Rev. Gerald Joseph, O.M.C., J.C.D., The Third Order Secular of Saint Francis, 201 pp., 1928.
51. Schenk, Rev. Francis J., J.C.D., The Matrimonial Impediments of Mixed Religion and Disparity of Cult, XVI-318 pp., 1929.
52. Coady, Rev. John Joseph, S.T.D., J.U.D., A.M., The Appointment of Pastors, VIII-150 pp., 1929.
53. Kay, Thomas Henry, J.C.D., Competence in Matrimonial Procedure, VIII-164 pp., 1929.
54. Turner, Rev. Sidney Joseph, C.P., J.U.D., The Vow of Poverty, XLIX-217 pp., 1929.
55. Kearney, Rev. Raymond A., A.B., S.T.D., J.C.D., The Principles of Delegation, VII-149 pp., 1929.
56. Conran, Rev. Edward James, A.B., J.C.D., The Interdict, V-163 pp., 1930.
57. O'Neil, Rev. William H., J.C.D., Papal Rescripts of Favor, VII-218 pp., 1930.
58. Bastnagel, Rev. Clement Vincent, J.U.D., The Appointment of Parochial Adjutants and Assistants, XV-257 pp., 1930.
59. Ferry, Rev. William A., A.B., J.C.D., Stole Fees, V-135 pp., 1930.
60. Costello, Rev. John Michael, A.B., J.C.D., Domicile and Quasi-Domicile, VII-201 pp., 1930.
61. Kremer, Rev. Michael Nicholas, A.B., S.T.B., J.C.D., Church Support in the United States, VI-1930.
62. Angulo, Rev. Luis, C.M., J.C.D., Legislación de la Iglesia sobre la intención en la aplicación de la Santa Misa, VII-104 pp., 1931.
63. Frey, Rev. Wolfgang Norbert, O.S.B., A.B., J.C.D., The Act of Religious Profession, VIII-174 pp., 1931.
64. Roberts, Rev. James Brendan, A.B., J.C.D., The Banns of Marriage, XIV-140 pp., 1931.
65. Ryder, Rev. Raymond Aloysius, A.B., J.C.D., Simony, IX-151 pp., 1931.
66. Campagna, Rev. Angelo, Ph.D., J.U.D., Il Vicario Generale del Vescovo, VII-205 pp., 1931.

67. Cox, Rev. Joseph Godfrey, A.B., J.C.D., The Administration of Seminaries, VI-124 pp., 1931.
68. Gregory, Rev. Donald J., J.U.D., The Pauline Privilege, XV-165 pp., 1931.
69. Donohue, Rev. John F., J.C.D., The Impediment of Crime, VII-110 pp., 1931.
70. Dooley, Rev. Eugene A., O.M.I., J.C.D., Church Law On Sacred Relics, IX-143 pp., 1931.
71. Orth, Rev. Raymond Clement, O.M.C., J.C.D., The Approbation of Religious Institutes, 171 pp., 1931.
72. Pernicone, Rev. Joseph M., A.B., J.C.D., The Ecclesiastical Prohibition of Books, XII-267 pp., 1932.
73. Clinton, Rev. Connell, A.B., J.C.D., The Paschal Precept, IX-108 pp., 1932.
74. Donnelly, Rev. Francis B., A.M., S.T.L., J.C.D., The Diocesan Synod, VIII-125 pp., 1932.
75 Torrente, Rev. Camilo, C.M.F., J.C.D., Las Processiones Sagradas, V-145 pp., 1932.
76. Murphy, Rev. Edwin J., C.PP.S., J.C.D., Suspension Ex Informata Conscientia, XI-122 pp., 1932.
77. Mackenzie, Rev. Eric F., A.M., S.T.L., J.C.D., The Delict of Heresy in its Commission, Penalization, Absolution, VII-124 pp., 1932.
78. Lyons, Rev. Avitus E., S.T.B., The Collegiate Tribunal of First Instance, XI-147 pp., 1932.
79. Connolly, Rev. Thomas A., J.C.D., Appeals, XI-195 pp., 1932.
80. Sangmeister, Rev. Joseph V., A.B., J.C.D., Force and Fear as Precluding Matrimonial Consent, V-211 pp., 1932.
81. Jaeger, Rev. Leo A., A.B., J.C.D., The Administration of Vacant and Quasi-Vacant Episcopal Sees in the United States, IX-229 pp., 1932.
82. Rimlinger, Rev. Herbert T., J.C.D., Error Invalidating Matrimonial Consent, VII-79 pp., 1932.
83. Barrett, Rev. John D. M., S.S., J.C.D., A Comparative Study of the Third Plenary Council of Baltimore and the Code, IX-221 pp., 1932.
84. Carberry, Rev. John J., Ph.D., S.T.D., J.C.D., The Juridical Form of Marriage, X-177 pp., 1934.
85. Dolan, Rev. John L., A.B., J.C.D., The Defensor Vinculi, XII-157 pp., 1934.
86. Hannan, Rev. Jerome D., A.M., S.T.D., LL.B., J.C.D., The Canon Law of Wills, IX-517 pp., 1934.
87. Lemieux, Rev. Delisle A., A.M., J.C.D., The Sentence in Ecclesiastical Procedure, IX-131 pp., 1934.
88. O'Rourke, Rev. James J., A.B., J.C.D., Parish Registers, VII-109 pp., 1934.
89. Timlin, Rev. Bartholomew, O.F.M., A.M., J.C.D., Conditional Matrimonial Consent, X-381 pp., 1934.

90. Wahl, Rev. Francis X., A.B., J.C.D., The Matrimonial Impediments of Consanguinity and Affinity, VI-125 pp., 1934.
91. White, Rev. Robert J., A.B., LL.B., S.T.B., J.C.D., Canonical Ante-Nuptial Promises and the Civil Law, VI-152 pp., 1934.
92. Herrera, Rev. Antonio Parra, O.C.D., J.C.D., Legislación Ecclesiástica sobre el Ayuno y la Abstinencia, XI-191 pp., 1935.
93. Kennedy, Rev. Edwin J., J.C.D., The Special Matrimonial Process in Cases of Evident Nullity, X-165 pp., 1935.
94. Manning, Rev. John J., A.B., J.C.D., Presumption of Law in Matrimonial Procedure, XI-111 pp., 1935.
95. Moeder, Rev. John M., J.C.D., The Proper Bishop for Ordination and Dimissorial Letters, VII-135 pp., 1935.
96. O'Mara, Rev. William A., A.B., J.C.D., Canonical Causes for Matrimonial Dispensations, IX-155 pp., 1935.
97. Reilly, Rev. Peter, J.C.D., Residence of Pastors, IX-81 pp., 1935.
98. Smith, Rev. Mariner T., O.P., S.T.L., J.C.D., The Penal Law for Religious, VII-169 pp., 1935.
99. Whalen, Rev. Donald W., A.M., J.C.D., The Value of Testimonial Evidence in Matrimonial Procedure, XIII-297 pp., 1935.
100. Cleary, Rev. Joseph F., J.C.D., Canonical Limitations on the Alienation of Church Property, VIII-141 pp., 1936.
101. Glynn, Rev. John C., J.C.D., The Promoter of Justice, XX-337 pp., 1936.
102. Brennan, Rev. James H., S.S., A.M., S.T.B., J.C.D., The Simple Convalidation of Marriage, VI-135 pp., 1937.
103. Brunini, Rev. Joseph Bernard, J.C.D., The Clerical Obligations of Canons 139 and 142, X-121 pp., 1937.
104. Connor, Rev. Maurice, A.B., J.C.D., The Administrative Removal of Pastors, VIII-159 pp., 1937.
105. Guilfoyle, Rev. Merlin Joseph, J.C.D., Custom, XI-144 pp., 1937.
106. Hughes, Rev. James Austin, A.B.; A.M., J.C.D., Witnesses in Criminal Trials of Clerics, IX-140 pp., 1937.
107. Jansen, Rev. Raymond J., A.B., S.T.L., J.C.D., Canonical Provisions for Catechetical Instruction, VII-153 pp., 1937.
108. Kealy, Rev. John James, A.B., J.C.D., The Introductory Libellus in Church Court Procedure, XI-121 pp., 1937.
109. McManus, Rev. James Edward, C.SS.R., J.C.D., The Administration of Temporal Goods in Religious Institutes, XVI-196 pp., 1937.
110. Moriarity, Rev. Eugene James, J.C.D., Oaths in Ecclesiastical Courts, X-115 pp., 1937.
111. Rainer, Rev. Eligius George, C.SS.R., J.C.D., Suspension of Clerics, XVII-249 pp., 1937.
112. Reilly, Rev. Thomas F., C.SS.R., J.C.D., Visitation of Religious, VI-195 pp., 1938.
113. Moriarty, Rev. Francis E., C.SS.R., J.C.D., The Extraordinary Absolution from Censures, XV-334 pp., 1938.

114. Connolly, Rev. Nicholas P., J.C.D., The Canonical Erection of Parishes, X-132 pp., 1938.
115. Donovan, Rev. James Joseph, J.C.D., The Pastor's Obligation in Prenuptial Investigation, XII-322 pp., 1938.
116. Harrigan, Rev. Robert J., M.A., S.T.B., J.C.D., The Radical Sanation of Invalid Marriages, VIII-208 pp., 1938.
117. Boffa, Rev. Conrad Humbert, J.C.D., Canonical Provisions for Catholic Schools, X-211 pp., 1939.
118. Parsons, Rev. Anscar John, O.F.M. Cap., J.C.D., Canonical Elections, XII-236 pp., 1939.
119. Reilly, Rev. Edward Michael, A.B., J.C.D., The General Norms of Dispensation, X-156 pp., 1939.
120. Ryan, Rev. Gerald Aloysius, A.B., J.C.D., Principles of Episcopal Jurisdiction, XII-172 pp., 1939.
121. Burton, Rev. Francis James, C.S.C., A.B., J.C.D., A Commentary on Canon 1125, X-222 pp., 1940.
122. Miaskiewicz, Rev. Francis Sigismund, J.C.D., Supplied Jurisdiction According to Canon 209, XII-340 pp., 1940.
123. Rice, Rev. Patrick William, A.B., J.C.D., Proof of Death in Prenuptial Investigation, VIII-156 pp., 1940.
124. Anglin, Rev. Thomas Francis, M.S., J.C.D., The Eucharistic Fast, VIII-183 pp., 1941.
125. Coleman, Rev. John Jerome, J.C.D., The Minister of Confirmation, VI-153 pp., 1941.
126. Downs, Rev. John Emmanuel, A.B., J.C.D., The Concept of Clerical Immunity, XI-163 pp., 1941.
127. Esswein, Rev. Anthony Albert, J.C.D., Extrajudicial Penal Powers of Ecclesiastical Superiors, X-144 pp., 1941.
128. Farrell, Rev. Benjamin Francis, M.A., S.T.L., J.C.D., The Rights and Duties of the Local Ordinary Regarding Congregations of Women Religious of Pontifical Approval, V-195 pp., 1941.
129. Feeney, Rev. Thomas John, A.B., S.T.L., J.C.D., Restitutio in Integrum, VI-169 pp., 1941.
130. Findlay, Rev. Stephen William, O.S.B., A.B., J.C.D., Canonical Norms Governing the Deposition and Degradation of Clerics, XVII-279 pp., 1941.
131. Goodwine, Rev. John, A.B., S.T.L., J.C.D., The Right of the Church to Acquire Property, VIII-119 pp., 1941.
132. Heston, Rev. Edward Louis, C.S.C., Ph.D., S.T.D., J.C.D., The Alienation of Church Property in the United States, XII-222 pp., 1941.
133. Hogan, Rev. James John, A.B., S.T.L., J.C.D., Judicial Advocates and Procurators, VIII-200 pp., 1941.
134. Kealy, Rev. Thomas M., A.B., Litt.B., J.C.D., Dowry of Women Religious, IX-152 pp., 1941.
135. Keene, Rev. Michael James, O.S.B., J.C.D., Religious Ordinaries and Canon 198.

136. Kerin, Rev. Charles A., S.S., M.A., S.T.B., J.C.D., The Privation of Christian Burial, XVI-279 pp., 1941.
137. Louis, Rev. William Francis, M.A., J.C.D., Diocesan Archives, X-101 pp., 1941.
138. McDevitt, Rev. Gilbert Joseph, A.B., J.C.D., Legitimacy and Legitimation, X-247 pp., 1941.
139. McDonough, Rev. Thomas Joseph, A.B., J.C.D., Apostolic Administrators, X-217 pp., 1941.
140. Meier, Rev. Carl Anthony, A.B., J.C.D., Penal Administrative Procedure Against Negligent Pastors, XI-240 pp., 1941.
141. Schmidt, Rev. John Rogg, A.B., J.C.D., The Principles of Authentic Interpretation in Canon 17 of the Code of Canon Law, XII-331 pp., 1941.
142. Slafkosky, Rev. Andrew Leonard, A.B., J.C.D., The Canonical Episcopal Visitation of the Diocese, X-197 pp., 1941.
143. Swoboda, Rev. Innocent Robert, O.F.M., J.C.D., Ignorance in Relation to the Imputability of Delicts, IX-271 pp., 1941.
144. Dubé, Rev. Arthur Joseph, A.B., J.C.D., The General Principles for the Reckoning of Time in Canon Law, VIII-299 pp., 1941.
145. McBride, Rev. James T., A.B., J.C.D., Incardination and Excardination of Seculars, XX-585 pp., 1941.
146. Król, Rev. John J., J.C.L., The Defendant in Contentious Trials.
147. Comyns, Rev. Joseph J., C.SS.R., J.C.L., The Papal and Episcopal Administration of Church Property.
148. Barry, Rev. Garrett Francis, O.M.I., J.C.L., Violation of the Cloister.
149. Bolduc, Rev. Gatien, C.S.V., A.B., S.T.L., J.C.L., Les études dans les religions cléricales.
150. Boyle, Rev. David John, M.A., J.C.L., The Juridic Effects of Moral Certitude on Pre-Nuptial Guarantees.
151. Canavan, Rev. Walter Joseph, M.A., Litt.D., J.C.L., The Profession of Faith.
152. Desrochers, Rev. Bruno, A.B., Ph.L., S.T.B., J.C.L., Le Premier Concile Plénier de Québec et le Code de Droit Canonique.
153. Dillon, Rev. Robert Edward, A.B., J.C.L., Common Law Marriage.
154. Dodwell, Rev. Edward John, Ph.D., S.T.B., J.C.L., The Time and Place for the Celebration of Marriage.
155. Donnellan, Rev. Thomas Andrew, A.B., J.C.L., The Obligation of the Missa pro Populo.
156. Eltz, Rev. Louis Anthony, A.B., J.C.L., Cooperators in Crimes According to Canon 2209.
157. Gass, Rev. Sylvester, Francis, M.A., J.C.L., Ecclesiastical Pensions.
158. Guiniven, Rev. John Joseph, C.SS.R., J.C.L., The Precept of Hearing Mass on Sundays and Holy Days of Obligation.
159. Gulczynski, Rev. John Theophilus, J.C.L., The Desecration and Violation of Churches.

160. Hammill, Rev. John Leo, M.A., J.C.L., The Obligations of the Traveler according to Canon 14.
161. Haydt, Rev. John Joseph, A.B., J.C.L., Reserved Benefices.
162. Huser, Rev. Roger John, O.F.M., A.B., J.C.L., The Canonical Crime of Abortion.
163. Kearney, Rev. Francis Patrick, A.B., S.T.L., J.C.L., The Principles of Canon 1127.
164. Linahen, Rev. Leo James, S.T.L., J.C.L., De Absolutione Complicis In Peccato Turpi.
165. McCloskey, Rev. Joseph Aloysius, A.B., J.C.L., The Subject of Ecclesiastical Law according to Canon 12.
166. O'Neill, Rev. Francis Joseph, C.SS.R., J.C.L., The Dismissal of Religious in Temporary Vows.
167. Prince, Rev. John Edward, A.B., S.T.B., J.C.L., The Diocesan Chancellor.
168. Riesner, Rev. Albert Joseph, C.SS.R., J.C.L., Apostates and Fugitives from Religious Institutes.
169. Stenger, Rev. Joseph Bernard, J.C.L., The Mortgaging of Church Property.
170. Waldron, Rev. Joseph Francis, A.B., J.C.L., The Minister of Baptism.
171. Willett, Rev. Robert Albert, J.C.L., The Probative Value of Documents in Ecclesiastical Trials.
172. Woeber, Rev. Edward Martin, M.A., J.C.L., The Interpellations.

www.ingramcontent.com/pod-product-compliance
Lightning Source LLC
LaVergne TN
LVHW050220080826
844660LV00012B/444

* 9 7 8 0 8 1 3 2 2 3 5 0 6 *